Y0-ASL-977

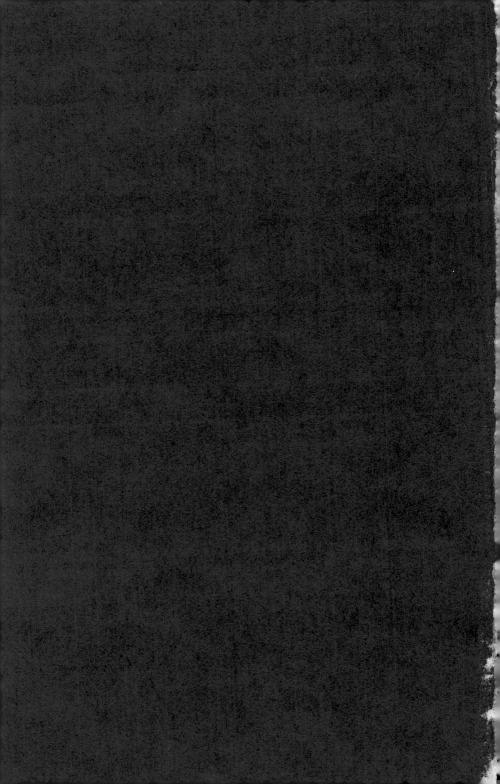

Motorsports

SPORTS, GAMES, AND PASTIMES INFORMATION GUIDE SERIES

Series Editor: Ronald M. Ziegler, Humanities Reference Librarian, Holland Reference Library, Washington State University, Pullman

Also in this series:

BICYCLING—*Edited by Mark P. Schultz and Barbara A. Schultz**

CAMPING AND BACKPACKING—*Edited by Cecil F. Clotfelter and Mary L. Clotfelter**

GAMBLING—*Edited by Jack I. Gardner**

GARDENING AND HOME LANDSCAPING—*Edited by Michel Michelsen**

GOLF—*Edited by Joseph S.F. Murdoch and Janet Seagle**

HORSEMANSHIP—*Edited by Ellen B. Wells*

PRIVATE AVIATION—*Edited by Floyd Nester Reister*

RACKET AND PADDLE GAMES—*Edited by David Peele**

WILDERNESS WATERWAYS—*Edited by Ronald M. Ziegler*

WINTER SPORTS—*Edited by Diane C. Balodis**

WOMEN IN SPORTS—*Edited by Mary L. Remley**

*in preparation

The above series is part of the
GALE INFORMATION GUIDE LIBRARY

The Library consists of a number of separate series of guides covering major areas in the social sciences, humanities, and current affairs.

General Editor: Paul Wasserman, Professor and former Dean, School of Library and Information Services, University of Maryland

Managing Editor: Denise Allard Adzigian, Gale Research Company

Motorsports

A GUIDE TO INFORMATION SOURCES

Volume 5 in the Sports, Games, and Pastimes
Information Guide Series

Susan Ebershoff-Coles

Supervisor of Technical Services
Indianapolis-Marion County Public Library

Charla Ann Leibenguth

Science Librarian
Butler University
Indianapolis, Indiana

Gale Research Company
Book Tower, Detroit, Michigan 48226

Library of Congress Cataloging in Publication Data

Ebershoff-Coles, Susan.
Motorsports : a guide to information sources.

(Sports, games, and pastimes information guide series ; 5) (Gale information guide library)
Includes indexes.
1. Motorsports—Bibliography. I. Leibenguth, Charla, joint author. II. Title. III. Series.
Z7514.M68E2 [GV1019.2] 016.7967 79-13736
ISBN 0-8103-1446-0

For Our Parents

VITAE

Susan Ebershoff-Coles is currently supervisor of technical services at the Indianapolis-Marion County Public Library. A native of Lafayette, Indiana, she received her B.A. degree from Purdue University and has an M.L.S. in library science. She holds a national competition license from the Sports Car Club of America and is also a licensed official for the United States Auto Club (USAC). She normally works in timing and scoring for USAC at championship, dirt car, and stock car races. She also reviews for the LIBRARY JOURNAL and AMERICAN REFERENCE BOOKS ANNUAL and is a member of the Auto Racing Writers and Broadcasters Association.

Charla Leibenguth is currently science librarian at Butler University in Indianapolis where she also teaches a course in pharmaceutical literature. She received her B.S. and M.S. from Purdue University in pharmacy. She is a free-lance writer specializing in ecology, science, and auto racing. She is a member of the Auto Racing Writers and Broadcasters Association and reviews books for LIBRARY JOURNAL and AMERICAN REFERENCE BOOKS ANNUAL.

CONTENTS

Contents

PREFACE

This book is the fifth in the Sports, Games, and Pastimes Information Guide Series. The series embraces a diversity of literature on leisure activities. It may be axiomatic that when an individual is attracted to a sport or pastime, he or she longs to learn more about it, making a fertile spawning bed for specialized publications on the subject. Such publication possibilities do not languish unnoticed for long.

As a result, an announcement that there is a proliferation of sports and recreation literature hardly qualifies as news. However, it may be less obvious to those not associated with recreation research, subject-area collection building, and the publication of reference works in the field, that there has not been a concurrent development in sports and recreation bibliography to accurately record this growth. This series of information guides represents an acknowledgment of the need for bibliographic control, and an attempt to impose that control through the identification of books and other information sources within a wide range of sports, games, and pastimes. Volumes in this series attempt to provide librarians, researchers, practitioners, and others with selective, annotated lists of books and other pertinent information.

MOTORSPORTS is the end product of an effort to gather a vast amount of recent bibliographical and other information on land vehicles propelled by internal combustion engines (excluding snowmobiles which will be covered in a subsequent volume in the series). The book brings together material on vehicles ranging from Indy cars to go-karts. There is an extensive chapter on motorcycle racing, and another on recreational motorsports--including rallying and all-terrain vehicles.

Sources for obtaining films and other nonprint media are identified. Finally, there are directories of racing organizations as well as the publishers and distributors of motorsports books.

Preface

The combined effort of Susan Ebershoff-Coles and Charla Leibenguth has resulted in this timely and useful volume which should become a primary reference source for all who seek information on motorsports.

Ronald Ziegler, Series Editor
Washington State University

INTRODUCTION

Men have been competing against each other and against time in one form or another since the dawn of mankind. An inevitable outgrowth of the invention of engines was the matching of one against another and motorsports were born. The advent of the internal combustion engine opened a whole new realm of possibility which greatly appealed to some very innovative gentlemen and the race was on! It hasn't stopped since.

Motorsports are the children of technology and ingenuity, and the history of motor racing, in all its forms, is rife with men of the technological genius evident in the twentieth century. Daimler, Bugatti, Norton, Renault, Chevrolet, Porsche, Ferrari, Deusenberg, Ford, Chrysler, Dodge, Honda--these are only a very few of the men who created and built what has become one of the most popular spectator sports in the world. In the United States, auto racing draws more people than any sport other than horse racing and pari-mutuel betting. The Indianapolis 500 is the largest spectator event in the world.

It is reasonable, then, to assume that so popular an activity would have a large body of literature grow up around it. And so it has. Many excellent books and articles have been written about motor racing in all forms, particularly auto racing. We have attempted to assemble a substantial portion of that literature published since 1965. However, there are a few older titles, usually historical or biographical, which we felt should be included in any work of this type.

Only English-language materials are cited. Some of the cited titles are out of print but are available through interlibrary loan. The section on newsletters was particularly difficult to assemble as many of these items are published irregularly, ceased publication, or change title and format frequently. These newsletters do, however, represent an important segment of the contemporary motorsports literature and deserve to be considered. All were in existence as of this writing unless otherwise noted. Specific articles published in periodicals have not been included.

Introduction

Motor racing tends to develop in regional pockets where local racing groups are very active and we have attempted to locate as many of these areas as possible.

Motorsports literature owes a great debt to British writers and publishers. Many of the cited British publications are available in the United States from Haessner Publishing and International Motorbooks (see the chapter "Publishers and Distributors" for addresses).

We wish to thank the many organizations, publishers, and distributors who have provided us with review copies and other pertinent information. Without their help our work would have been much more difficult.

Susan Ebershoff-Coles
Charla Leibenguth

Chapter 1

AUTO RACING

Of all the aspects of motorsports, auto racing has the largest body of available information. The first section comprises all material which involves more than one area of auto racing. Also included are topics for which only one book was available. The other sections are more specific so each deals with a separate topic. Some of the cited works are out of print but were considered important enough to be included. We were unable to inspect a few of these materials, but we have included them because the prominence of the authors and the relevance of the subject matter suggest their importance.

A. BACKGROUND AND GENERAL WORKS

Alexander, Jesse. AT SPEED. Introduction by Karl [E.] Ludvigsen. Newport Beach, Calif.: Bond, Parkhurst Publications, 1972. 158 p. Photos by Jesse Alexander.

> This book is a brief history of auto racing and the men who were a part of it.

Ayling, Keith. GAS, GUTS AND GLORY: GREAT MOMENTS IN INTERNATIONAL AUTO RACING. New York: Abelard-Schuman, 1970. 242 p. Index. Illus.

> Ayling discusses some of the great races, the cars competing in them, and the drivers who raced them. There is a chapter on driving as a career.

Ball, Adrian, ed. MY GREATEST RACE: BY TWENTY OF THE FINEST MOTOR RACING DRIVERS OF ALL TIME. New York: E.P. Dutton and Co., 1974. 139 p. B/w photos.

> This book, written for the Jim Clark Foundation, spans the time from Philippe Etancelin's description of the 1930 French Grand Prix up to Emerson Fittipaldi's exciting 1973 Argentine Grand Prix. Race courses from the Mille Miglia to the Indianapolis 500 are explored and drivers from Baron Huschke von Hanstein

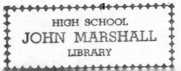

to the great Fangio are quoted. The book will be a bit of a disappointment for anyone hoping for deep insights into a driver's soul, but it does provide pleasant reading.

Bochroch, Albert R. AMERICAN AUTOMOBILE RACING: AN ILLUSTRATED HISTORY. New York: Viking, 1974. 260 p. Appendix. Photos.

The complete story of American automobile racing, from its beginning in 1895 to 1973, is documented in this book. Photographs and an appendix listing major race winners from 1895 to 1972 supplement the text. The book includes all types of racing, and is the most comprehensive history of U.S. racing available.

Boddy, William. THE HISTORY OF MOTOR RACING. New York: G.P. Putnam's Sons, 1977. 316 p. Index. Col. and b/w photos.

This book would be more appropriately titled "History of European Road Racing" since Boddy covers very little on racing other than road racing. He has done an excellent job of covering road racing from the earliest "Reliability Trial" of 1894 to the 1976 Grand Prix championship. Cars, drivers, circuits, and organizations are all discussed. The book has 350 photographs, 170 of which are in color and includes maps of all current Grand Prix circuits, tables of race winners, record breakers and world champions, and a description of Grand Prix formulae, 1906-77.

Borgeson, Griffith. THE GOLDEN AGE OF THE AMERICAN RACING CAR. New York: W.W. Norton, 1966. 288 p. Index. Appendixes. Photos.

Borgeson has produced an excellent work dealing with the period from about 1910 to 1929. He talks about the early days of American motor racing, the beginning of the AAA Contest Board, and the men who made it go. The section on the board tracks, how they were built and how they were driven, makes fascinating reading. Four of the greats of the age, Fred Duesenberg, Louis Chevrolet, Harry Miller, and Leo Goossen are discussed at length. The decade of the roaring twenties is also fully discussed along with such topics as the Frontenac, front wheel drive, Frank Lockhart, Jimmy Murphy's Grand Prix win, and the futurist Packard. Five appendixes are included. The first, giving the location, designer, length, and years active of the board tracks, is the most interesting.

Brittan, Nick, ed. MOTOR RACING: THE INTERNATIONAL WAY. NUMBER 1. New York: A.S. Barnes and Co., 1970. 120 p. Glossary. Illus.

This is a collection of eighteen articles written by experts in the world of auto racing, including the pieces written by drivers Jackie Stewart, Bruce McLaren, Gerry Birrell, and John Miles. A racing marshall describes his work; there is a biography of Australian Tim

Schenken, a Formula 3 driver; an article on the world of rallying; and a glossary of race terms. An interesting entry in motorsports literature.

______. MOTOR RACING: THE INTERNATIONAL WAY. NUMBER 2. New York: A.S. Barnes and Co., 1972. 88 p. Illus.

This is a collection of thirteen articles on a variety of racing topics. Included are subjects such as "A Week in the Life of a Formula I Mechanic," Jackie Stewart, European hill climbs, Formula Ford, the Chaparral 2J, and others.

Butler, Hal. ROAR OF THE ROAD: THE STORY OF AUTO RACING. New York: Julian Messner, 1969. 224 p. Index.

A brief history of auto racing, this book covers the early races, the Grand Prix circuit, the sports car circuit, oval track racing, and briefly touches on stock car, midget, and drag racing.

Butterworth, W.E. AN ALBUM OF AUTOMOBILE RACING. New York: Franklin Watts, 1977. 96 p. Index. Illus., b/w photos.

Butterworth discusses the history of automobile racing with emphasis on early twentieth-century races and the development of race cars. The illustrations are the strongest part of a rather weak book; many are black-and-white photographs of early events and cars. The book is aimed at a younger audience.

Carlsen, Ruth Christoffer, and Carlsen, G. Robert, eds. THE GREAT AUTO RACE AND OTHER STORIES OF MEN AND CARS. New York: Scholastic Book Services, 1965. 124 p.

A series of articles and stories previously printed in magazines and now collected under one cover, this material is split evenly between fiction and nonfiction and includes articles on Nuvolari, Stirling Moss, and the Stanley Steamer. The reading is easy but interesting and the book is a good addition to the young adult collection.

Cooper-Evans, Michael, and Surtees, John. SIX DAYS IN AUGUST. London: Pelham Books, 1968. 133 p. Illus.

Del Valle, Julio Toledo. CARS ON ROAD AND TRACK. New York: Sterling Publishing Co., 1972. 112 p. Index. Col. and b/w photos.

A small book, this volume has a good deal of common superficial material packed into it. The book attempts to be a jack-of-all information particularly in the sports car field. There is a history of the invention of the automobile, a bit on the land speed record, and some easily understood chapters explaining car engines, transmissions, and chassis. The most helpful parts of the book are a chapter devoted to car makes and one to famous racing circuits. This book merely skims the surface of racing--everything in it can be found elsewhere in more detail.

Dugdale, John. GREAT MOTOR SPORT OF THE THIRTIES: A PERSONAL ACCOUNT. New York: Two Continents, 1977. 256 p. Photos.

Dugdale, an experienced automotive journalist and former editor of the British magazine AUTOCAR, gives a first hand account of racing and race results from all over the world. Emphasis is European, but he touches briefly on the American racing scene, including Whitney Straight's Indianapolis-built Duesenberg and John Cobb's land speed record runs on the Bonneville Salt Flats. His discussions of the Big Four of Grand Prix racing in this period, Mercedes, Auto Union, Alfa Romeo, and Maserati, are particularly interesting. The drivers of this era were excellent and Dugdale knew them all. A fine contribution to the literature.

Dymock, Eric. THE WORLD OF RACING CARS. London: Hamlyn, 1972. 128 p. Index. Col. and b/w photos.

Dymock provides a look at modern motorsport and the developments which led to today's cars and drivers. The emphasis is on European and sports car racing with occasional mention of the Indianapolis 500 and the Offenhauser engine. One chapter is devoted to the great names in racing such as Ferrari, Lotus, Porsche, BRM, and Cosworth. A chapter on great drivers includes Jimmy Clark, Jackie Stewart, Fangio, Stirling Moss, and Graham Hill. A chapter entitled "Ladder to the Top" gives a brief view of the usual steps a driver must take to step into a Formula I car.

Engel, Lyle Kenyon. ROAD RACING IN AMERICA. New York: Dodd, Mead and Co., 1971. 146 p. Glossary.

Engel details the fluctuating fortunes of American road racing and the current growing popularity of this form of racing. The book covers SCCA, Grand Prix racing in the United States, Trans-American, and Indy cars on road courses.

Flower, Raymond. MOTOR SPORTS: A PICTORIAL HISTORY. New York: G.P. Putnam's Sons, 1975. 240 p. Index. Appendixes.

Flower traces the history of racing in words and pictures from Paris in 1887 to the present. All types of racing are covered including the Gordon Bennett Cup, the Peking to Paris marathon, Brooklands, Grand Prix, Land Speed Records, and Indianapolis. A results appendix gives valuable reference material on famous races listing winning cars and drivers from the beginning to 1974. Also valuable is an appendix that gives track diagrams for various tracks and closed road circuits including several that are not easily found in racing books.

Fox, Charles. THE GREAT RACING CARS AND DRIVERS. New York: Grosset and Dunlap, 1972. 252 p.

Fox has picked his topics to show the evolution of the racing car and driver. He covers Pete DePaolo and his Duesenberg, the Bentley, Nuvolari, the roadster at Indy, the duels between Fangio and Moss, Phil Hill, Jimmy Clark, McLaren, and Jackie Stewart. The writing is good but overshadowed by the magnificent visual effects.

Garrett, Richard. THE MOTOR RACING STORY. Ist U.S. ed. New York: A.S. Barnes and Co., 1970. 196 p. Photos.

Garrett has written a general history of European motor racing with emphasis on people and the races rather than technical aspects of the cars. There is no index.

Georgano, G.N. A MOTOR RACING CAMERA, 1894-1916. North Pomfret, Vt.: David and Charles, 1976. 104 p. Photos.

This is a fascinating collection of old racing photographs, each well explained by a detailed annotation. Many of the prints were taken from the archives of the National Motor Museum and have never before been published. The photographs cover early town-to-town races, the Gordon Bennets, Grand Prixs, hillclimbs, and the beginning of racing at banked tracks such as Brooklands in England and Indianapolis in the United States.

______. A SOURCE BOOK OF RACING AND SPORTS CARS. London: Ward Lock, 1974. 144 p. Illus.

Georgano covers the development and engineering changes of the racing car. Over one hundred cars built between 1899 and 1972 are described and illustrated. This is an excellent survey of racing and sports machinery.

Green, Evan. EVAN GREEN'S WORLD OF MOTOR SPORT. London: Hamlyn, 1977. 206 p. Illus.

This is a volume of motorsport fact that covers rallying and Grand Prix among other material. It contains the results of all major racing and rallying series in Australia in 1976. It also has an article on motorsports in New Zealand.

Harding, Anthony, ed. THE RACERS AND DRIVER'S READER. New York: Arco Publishing Co., 1972. 294 p. Photos.

An anthology of articles about cars, this book has something for every car buff. Grand Prix, rallying, and the technical side of racing are covered along with bonus touches of verse, science fiction, cartoons, and some excellent photographs. Contributors include Paul Frere, Denis Jenkinson, David Hodges, and Eoin Young. Well edited and well written, motor nuts will enjoy it.

Hassan, Walter, in collaboration with Graham Robson. CLIMAX IN COVENTRY: MY LIFE OF FINE ENGINES AND FAST CARS. Minneapolis: Motorbooks International, 1977. 158 p. Photos.

Hassan has made notable contributions to the design and development of high performance cars and engines with this work. Some of the cars discussed include Bentley, Barnato, Pacey, Wilkins, Bristol, ERA, Railton, BRM, Jaguar, and Coventry Climax. Interesting technical descriptions of the cars are included.

Helck, Peter. THE CHECKERED FLAG. New York: Charles Scribner's Sons, 1961. 178 p.

Helck traces the history of early auto racing from its beginning to the end of the classic era in 1916. The Vanderbilt Cup races, the Bennett races, early road races, and the Grand Prize races are recounted in detail.

______. GREAT AUTO RACES. New York: Harry N. Abrams, 1975. 266 p. Index. Illus.

A monumental collection of drawings and paintings done by the author with descriptions of the cars and events depicted in the paintings, this expensive book is destined to become a collectors item. Nearly every phase of racing is done with heavy emphasis on early racing in Europe and the United States. Many famous paintings are reproduced here including "Vladivostok Mud" depicting the American Thomas crew hauling the Prussian Protos out of the mud during the 1908 New York-Paris event and "Gallant Defeat" portraying Ralph De Palma and Jenkins pushing their disabled Mercedes across the finish line during the 1912 Indianapolis 500. This is an excellent book with beautiful illustrations.

Hill, Graham. GRAHAM HILL'S CAR RACING GUIDE. New York: Sterling Publishing Co., 1971. 76 p. Index. Photos.

Hill's book contains basic descriptions of a race, the type of person who is a racing driver, types of racing cars and circuits. There are profiles of famous drivers, most of whom are no longer active. One chapter is devoted to racing terms.

Holliday, Bob. RACING ROUND THE ISLAND: A MANX TALE OF SPEED ON WHEELS. North Pomfret, Vt.: David and Charles, 1976. 212 p. Index.

In 1904 racing began on the Isle of Man and this book is a history of the cars and motorcycles that have brought fame to the island since that fateful day. Holliday has filled a gap in racing history with his narration of how the sport grew through the years--Gordon Bennett, Tourist Trophy races, Bicycle TT, rallying, karting. This is not a colorful history but one crammed with facts.

Hough, Richard, ed. FIRST AND FASTEST: A COLLECTION OF ACCOUNTS OF THE WORLD'S GREATEST AUTO RACES. New York: Harper and Row, 1964. 229 p. Photos., diags.

A collection of accounts of some of the greatest and most memorable races ever run. Each story was written by someone who was there. Some of the events included are the 1903 Paris-Madrid, 1906 Vanderbilt Cup, 1914 Tourist Trophy, the 1925 and 1963 Indianapolis 500, 1952 Le Mans, the 1955 Mille Miglia, and the 1958 Miglia di Monza. Each account is prefaced by some background information.

Hough, Richard, and Frostick, Michael. A HISTORY OF THE WORLD'S RACING CARS. New York: Harper and Row, 1965. 190 p. Index. Col. and b/w illus., line drwgs.

The author traces the growth and development of the sport from its beginning to 1965.

Howell, John. SEVENTY YEARS OF MOTORSPORTS. Worcester, Engl.: Littlebury, 1971. 88 p. Photos.

Howell reawakens memories of some of the great days in motorsports. He covers both auto racing and motorcycle racing.

Jackson, Robert B. RACING CARS. New York: Henry Z. Walck, 1970. 63 p. B/w photos.

Jackson briefly covers track racing cars like Indy cars, sprints, midget, and stock cars, straight line cars such as Land Speed Record machines and drag racers, all kinds of road racing cars and off-road racing cars. The book is acceptable for older children as well as some adults. There is no index.

Keyser, Michael. THE SPEED MERCHANTS. Englewood Cliffs, N.J.: Prentice-Hall, 1973. 176 p. Photos.

Keyser unfolds a look at Grand Prix and sports car racing today beginning with the machines, then the type of men generally and specifically who race these cars. There are many quotes from the people involved. Although not technical, the book does capture the flavor of the racing scene.

King, Brad. ALL COLOR BOOK OF RACING CARS. London: Octopus Books, 1973. 72 p. Col. photos.

Over one hundred captioned color photographs relate the history of racing cars from the early Constatt-Daimler, Rover, and Humber down to the Chaparral, McLaren, and Eagle.

Lurani, Giovanni. HISTORY OF THE RACING CAR: MAN AND MACHINE. New York: Thomas Y. Crowell Co., 1972. 319 p. Illus.

This is a history of auto racing from the Paris-Bordeaux-Paris race to today's sophisticated rear engine machinery. There is heavy emphasis on Grand Prix racing.

Macbeth, Graham. THE OBSERVER'S BOOK OF MOTORSPORT. London: Frederick Warne and Co., 1975. 192 p. Index. Illus.

This book discusses many aspects of motor racing with emphasis on Grand Prix racing.

McMaster, W.A. HISTORY OF MOTORSPORT IN IRELAND, 1903-1969. Belfast: Century Services, 1971. 83 p. Illus.

Miller, Jerry. FAST COMPANY: THE MEN AND MACHINES OF AMERICAN AUTO RACING. Chicago: Follett Publishing Co., 1972. 305 p. Glossary. B/w photos.

Miller has written a book that peeks and prods at all types and levels of American racing. With a clear knowing style, Miller sketches precise colorful pictures of the drivers and their machines. The book is divided into four well-handled sections, The Sport, The People, Places and Racers, and Indianapolis. Of exceptional interest are the pieces on Jungle Park, Larry Burton, Ralph Liguori, Jimmy Maguire, Jigger Sirois, George Eaton, and Lee Kunzman. Lack of an index is the only deficit.

Moss, Stirling. HOW TO WATCH MOTOR RACING. New York: Dodd, Mead and Co., 1975. 152 p. Index. Photos.

Written primarily for the dedicated road racing fan, Moss tells how to keep track of what goes on before, during, and after a motor race. He talks about pit signals, lap charts, timing, tire usage, and strategy. Races, cars, and drivers vary so much and weather can be a major factor so Moss presents ways to interpret these various factors to keep up with what is really happening and why. The book includes a chapter on rallying and discussions of what to watch for on a few of the major European circuits.

Nicholson, T.R. ADVENTURER'S ROAD. New York: Rinehart and Co., 1957. 235 p. Index. B/w photos.

This detailed account of the Pekin-Paris road trial of 1907 and the New York-Paris motor race of 1908 makes entertaining reading.

_____. RACING CARS AND RECORD BREAKERS, 1898-1921. CARS OF THE WORLD IN COLOR. New York: Macmillan Co., 1971. 169 p. Index. Col. drwgs.

The book contains ninety-six numbered colored drawings of early race cars. Matching numbered brief articles provide some technical data, racing successes and failures, and the fate of the model. The index is an alphabetical listing of car names.

Nye, Doug. GREAT MOMENTS IN SPORT: MOTOR RACING. London: Pelham Books, 1976. 176 p. Index. B/w photos.

Nye recreates some of the classic motor contests run through the years from 1914 to 1975. Boillot, Murphy, Lockhart, Nuvolari, Hawthorn, Moss, Fangio, and Stewart are only a few of the great names covered. Emphasis is heavily on Grand Prix racing. Only one of the seventeen chapters deals with American racing and that one covers Frank Lockhart's Indy win.

_____. INTERNATIONAL MOTOR RACING. New York: Thomas Y. Crowell Co., 1974. 93 p. Photos.

A general summary of international road racing, this book gives hints on how to watch a motor race. Nye gives brief histories of the cars, drivers, events, and the tracks.

_____. MOTOR RACING MAVERICKS. London: Batsford, 1974. 198 p. Index. Illus.

_____. RACING CAR ODDITIES. New York: Arco Publishing Co., 1975. 198 p.

Nye presents a potpourri of some of the strangest racing cars ever built. Some had six wheels, others had two engines, another had a sidecar. All types of powerplants were used--even gunpowder. The book is a tribute to man's inventiveness.

Olney, Ross [R.]. GREAT MOMENTS IN SPEED. Englewood Cliffs, N.J.: Prentice-Hall, 1970. 146 p.

This is an interesting if superficial look at some highlights of automobile racing. Most of the stories revolve around Indianapolis drivers but a few touch on Grand Prix and other forms of motor sport. Especially interesting is the short chapter on one-handed midget driver Allen Heath. The time span covered is from 1903 to 1968.

Olney, Ross [R.], and Bush, Chan. "Shooting Automobile Racing and Other Motor Sports." In their PHOTOGRAPHING ACTION SPORTS, pp. 41-52. New York: Franklin Watts, 1976.

This book contains an excellent chapter on photographing auto racing. Written for the amateur, advice is clearly presented and little foreknowledge is expected. Not only is the photographer instructed on which camera to use but also on the best place to shoot pictures, the advance preparation to make, and the type of clothes to wear.

Pomeroy, Laurence. EVOLUTION OF THE RACING CAR. London: William Kimber, 1966. 240 p. Photos., diags.

A look at the development, changes, and varying philosophies of race car design.

Posthumus, Cyril, CLASSIC RACING CARS. New York: Rand McNally and Co., 1977. 160 p. Col. and b/w photos. No index.

Posthumus describes forty outstanding racing cars which span seventy years of competition history. The profiles are done in depth and analyze the technical makeup of the machines. The personalities of designers are recreated as are some of the men who drove these cars. Cars included range from the 1906 Grand Prix Renault and the Auto Union D-type to the Indianapolis Lotus Ford and the Ferrari Fiat-12312T.

Powell, Al. ASTONISHING--AND TRUE--STORIES OF THE SPEEDWAY. New York: Julian Messner, 1977. 158 p.

This is a series of short, easy-to-read tales gathered from many different areas of racing. Anecdotes include a shattered race car buried on a beach after the driver was killed, a driver shaving as he drove a race, a go-kart driven around the world, and early black driver Rajo Jack. The book is not meant to be taken as serious racing literature, but it is entertaining.

______. STRANGE BUT TRUE AUTO RACING STORIES. New York: Scholastic Book Services, 1974. 105 p.

Written for the young adult, this is a collection of four-to-five-page anecdotes covering all areas of automobile racing. There are stories on Jim Hurtubise's determination to race again; on Elfrieda Mais, an early woman driver; and on Henry Ford racing a car across a frozen lake. The stories are light, fun reading.

Puleo, Nicole. ROAD RACING. Fearon Racing Series. Belmont, Calif.: Fearon Publishers, 1974. 47 p. Illus.

This book traces the development of road racing from its beginnings to circuit racing today. It discusses the Grand Prix, Trans-Am, Can-Am, and the L&M Continental 5000.

_____. TRACK RACING. Fearon Racing Series. Belmont, Calif.: Fearon Publishers, 1974. 47 p. Illus.

This booklet traces the evolution of the automobile and the emergence of auto racing, stressing USAC and NASCAR. It is written at a fifth-grade reading level.

Roberts, Peter. RACING CARS AND THE HISTORY OF MOTOR SPORT. London: Octopus Books, 1973. 144 p. Index. Col. and b/w photos.

Roberts traces the history of racing's development from 1894 to 1972. Most types of racing are included: Formula I, Formula II, sports car racing, endurance racing, land speed record attempts, and Indianapolis. Coverage is not in-depth, but comments are informative.

_____. THE SHELL BOOK OF EPIC MOTOR RACES. New York: Arco Publishing Co., 1964. 128 p. Appendixes. B/w photos.

A short book on ten famous races ranging in time from the Gordon Bennett Race of 1902 to the German Grand Prix of 1962. There are various appendixes including the winners of world championship races from 1950-62, the winners of the Twenty-Four Hours of Le Mans 1923-64, and the winners of the Mille Miglia from 1927 to 1957.

Sawyer, John. THE DUSTY HEROES. Speedway, Ind.: Carl Hungness Publishing, 1978. 304 p.

This is the story of auto racing on dirt tracks since 1960.

Schuster, George, with Mahoney, Tom. THE LONGEST AUTO RACE. New York: John Day Co., 1966. 160 p. B/w photos.

This is an account of the famous New York to Paris race of 1908 which was run by six cars and finally won by an American, Thomas Flyer. Coauthor George Schuster accompanied the winning car in its drive around the world and his memories make an interesting tale. There are many good historic photographs.

Scodwell, Tony. ROAD RACING . . . A COLLECTION OF PHOTOGRAPHS. Limited Edition Collection. Las Vegas: Creative Photography Publishers, 1977. B/w photos.

A spectacular collection of over 150 photographs, this book is road racing seen through the eye of a camera. Each book in this series has been numbered and signed by the author and is a collector's item.

Snowdon, Nigel, and Tuckey, Bill. THE ULTIMATE EXCITEMENT; THE MOTOR RACING PHOTOGRAPHY OF NIGEL SNOWDON. Sydney, Australia: Murray, 1967. 159 p.

An excellent collection of racing photographs with European emphasis, compiled by Bill Tuckey.

Stambler, Irwin. GREAT MOMENTS IN AUTO RACING. New York: Scholastic Book Services, 1968. 158 p. Glossary. Illus.

Ten chapters cover famous races at the most important tracks in the world--Nurburgring, Daytona, Monza, South Africa, Riverside, Mille Miglia, Mexico City, Indianapolis, Darlington, and LeMans. Stock, Grand Prix, championship, and sports car races are all covered as well as famous drivers such as Fangio, Phil Hill, Graham Hill, and Dan Gurney.

Stevenson, Peter. THE GREATEST DAYS OF RACING. New York: Charles Scribner's Sons, 1972. 180 p. B/w photos.

This is a simple, easy-to-read view of auto racing told from short sketches of various periods of the sport of speed. Among topics covered are the Gordon Bennett Races, the saga of the Bentleys, American dirt track racing, Peter Collins, Mike Hawthorn, Stirling Moss, and Steve McQueen. A special chapter is devoted to American World Champion, Phil Hill.

Stropus, Judith V. THE STROPUS GUIDE TO AUTO RACING TIMING AND SCORING. Modern Sports Car Series. New York: Sports Car Press, 1975. 124 p.

Stropus shows the hows, whys, and why nots of timing and scoring for an individual race team.

Twite, M.L. THE WORLD'S RACING CARS. 4th ed., rev. Garden City, N.Y.: Doubleday and Co., 1971. 191 p. Photos.

This is a small reference guide to racing cars, providing specifications on most of the top racing machines in the world. A photograph of each design is included along with a brief history of each form. Included are racing cars from Formulas I, II, III, USAC, Formula 5000, Formula Ford, Can-Am, NASCAR, and Saloon Cars.

Watson, Dick. THE GLORY ROAD. New York: Stadia Sports Publishing, 1973. 160 p. Glossary. Photos.

This book features profiles and photographs of the top racing stars, reviews of major races, and previews of the 1973 classic races. An interesting chapter deals with the importance of teamwork to a winning effort.

Reference

Cutter, Robert, and Findell, Bob. THE ENCYCLOPEDIA OF AUTO RACING GREATS. Englewood Cliffs, N.J.: Prentice-Hall, 1973. 675 p. Glossary. Photos.

This is one of the best collections of auto racing biographies yet published. Included are drivers, designers, mechanics, and engineers. Among the drivers included are the winners of every Grand Prix race, everyone who ever scored a world championship point, land speed record holders, as well as many American stars. A total of 550 biographies and over 450 photographs make up the volume. The biographies are more complete than those in most books of this type and are accurate and well written. The table of contents provides a quick look at those included. No page numbers are given since the book is alphabetically arranged. A revised and updated edition is needed but this book will not lose its value for many years.

Georgano, G.N. THE ENCYCLOPEDIA OF MOTOR SPORT. New York: Viking, 1971. 656 p. Index. Glossary. Illus., col. and b/w photos.

The main sections of this book cover the organization of motorsport, the circuits, rallies, races and hillclimbs, the cars, and a glossary of terms. Biographies of 360 drivers are given. The first section has articles on each of the Formulas, the major sanctioning bodies or more specialized aspects of the sport such as Autocross and Rallycross, Trials, and vintage car racing. All sections are alphabetical within themselves. A brief description of each circuit, race, rally, and car is provided but no addresses are given for the circuits. Chitty-Chitty Bang-Bang is included in the listing of cars but A.J. Foyt's Coyote is not. The glossary provides lengthy definitions and some illustrations. The index includes only names and terms which do not have a separate listing in the alphabetical sections. The book is strong on European racing and adequate on U.S. championship racing. It is weak on drag racing and other forms of U.S. racing.

Harding, Anthony, ed. CAR FACTS AND FEATS: A RECORD OF EVERYDAY MOTORING AND AUTOMOTIVE ACHIEVEMENT. Garden City, N.Y.: Doubleday and Co., 1971. 256 p. Index.

Despite its title, this volume on auto racing is crammed full of little-known and well-known details about all forms of racing--historical, road racing (races, cars, and drivers), hill climbs and rallies, and track records. Each topic is covered in only a few lines. The excellent index makes this a valuable reference tool.

Pritchard, Anthony, and Davey, Keith. THE ENCYCLOPAEDIA OF MOTOR RACING. 2d ed. London: Hale, 1973. 377 p. Index. Illus.

This is an excellent reference source on cars, drivers, and events of international status.

Radosta, John S. THE NEW YORK TIMES COMPLETE GUIDE TO AUTO RACING. Chicago: Quadrangle Books, 1971. 256 p. Glossary.

A basic guide to auto racing, this book contains information on the clubs and organizations, the many types of cars, the tracks, rules, and a host of other information. Chapters on off-road racing, the economics of the sport, drag racing, road racing, and stock car racing, as well as USAC and Indianapolis coverage, present one of the best overviews of the entire sport available.

Yard, Larry L., and Brown, Allan E. NATIONAL SPEEDWAY DIRECTORY. 2d ed. Grand Rapids, Mich.: Dray Publishing, 1977. 447 p.

This pocket-size speedway directory provides detailed information on over nine hundred oval speedways and road courses located throughout the United States and Canada. It gives track names, directions to the tracks, phone numbers, names and addresses of promoters, size and surface type of each track, track records, and names and addresses of sanctioning bodies. It is very useful for locating some hard-to-find information.

Marques

Berry, Robert. JAGUAR: MOTOR RACING AND THE MANUFACTURER. Newfoundland, N.J.: Haessner, 1978. 72 p. Photos.

Berry relates the racing history of the Jaguar firm but this is little more than a dry recounting of facts. He gives an inside view of pit activities, corporate decision making, and engineering development as well as a look at the men who drove the Jaguars in competition.

Browing, Peter. THE WORKS MINIS; ILLUSTRATED HISTORY OF THE WORKS ENTERED MINIS IN INTERNATIONAL RALLIES AND RACES. Minneapolis: Motorbooks International, 1971. 206 p. Index. Illus.

Browing covers ten years of competition by the factory Mini team in races and rallies. A Mini buff will find the work a joy to read. There is an interesting chapter on the techniques of driving a Mini by Paddy Hopkirk, an internationally recognized rally driver.

Fahnestock, Murray. THE FAST FORD HANDBOOK. Arcadia, Calif.: Post Motor Books, 1968. 192 p. Photos., line drwgs.

Fahnestock has culled the best and most interesting of the information presented in a magazine series appearing in the pages of the

FORDOWNER. This series documented many of the very early speed efforts first tried on the Model T. These were contemporary accounts and emphasized the great variety of ideas and theories on the Model T as a speed car. This is an excellent source for authentic reproductions of this type of automobile.

Frankenberg, Richard von. PORSCHE: THE MAN AND HIS CARS. Translated by Charles Meisl. Cambridge, Mass.: Robert Bentley, 1961. 223 p.

A biography of a multifaceted man, Frankenberg relates the saga of Ferdinand Porsche from his birth in 1875 to his death in 1951. He briefly covers Porsche developments in auto racing up to 1959. Porsche was responsible not only for Porsche automobiles but for the original Volkswagen, tractors, tanks, and some of the finest racing machines ever built. An apolitical man, he, like Bugatti and others, was caught in the maelstrom of World War II and spent some time in prison.

Frere, Paul. THE RACING PORSCHES: A TECHNICAL TRIUMPH. New York: Arco Publishing Co., 1973. 212 p. Illus., charts, diags.

Frere begins with the relatively simple 6-cylinder machine and traces the history of the Porsche race cars into the 1972 version of the turbo-Porsche. There is much interesting information and technical details from previously guarded factory records.

Frostick, Michael, and Gill, Barrie. FORD COMPETITION CARS: THE FORD MOTOR COMPANY IN COMPETITION. Yeovil, Engl.: Haynes, 1976. 183 p. Index. Photos.

Frostick and Gill relate seventy years of competition effort by the Ford Motor Company. From the turn of the century, through two world wars and the highly successful years in the 1960s and 1970s. Ford's endeavors in rallies and races are discussed. The authors also cover the Formula I engine and Ford's efforts to win Le Mans and Indianapolis.

Grayson, Stan, ed. FERRARI: THE MAN, THE MACHINES. Princeton, N.J.: Princeton Publishing, 1975. 348 p. Index. Col. and b/w photos.

One cannot talk about European motor racing without talking about Ferrari. Both the man and his cars are living legends. Grayson has brought together excellent accounts of both by men who have known Ferrari and who have driven his cars. Phil Hill and Stirling Moss recount adventures in the cars and Griffith Borgeson reveals much about the complex man who is Enzo Ferrari. This is a book that all race enthusiasts will appreciate and Ferrari buffs will own.

Levine, Leo. FORD: THE DUST AND THE GLORY: A RACING HISTORY. London: Macmillan and Co., 1968. 630 p. Index. Illus.

This is a long, detailed, and well-written history of Ford Motor Company's involvement with motor racing. Indianapolis, Le Mans, the superspeedways of the southern stock car circuit, the Carrera Panamericana, drag cars, land speed record setters, all the glory is recounted by Levine. The men who built the cars, drove the cars, and served as mechanics for the cars are all represented. Levine provides one of the most detailed descriptions of racing action ever written.

Ludvigsen, Karl [E.]. GURNEY'S EAGLES: THE EXCITING STORY OF THE AAR RACING CARS. Minneapolis: Motorbooks International, 1976. 136 p. Index. B/w photos.

In 1964, with the help of Carroll Shelby and Goodyear Tire and Rubber Company, Dan Gurney formed All American Racers and the first of its Eagles roared to life in March of 1966. Since then the cars have competed successfully in Grand Prix, the Indianapolis 500, Formula 5000, and Can-Am racing. This is the story of the successes and failures, joys, and frustrations that made the car a legend. The designers, fabricators, mechanics, and drivers provide a who's who of contemporary racing. From 1966 to 1976 all the problems, innovations, wins, and losses are recounted.

______. THE MERCEDES-BENZ RACING CARS. Newport Beach, Calif.: Bond, Parkhurst Publications, 1971. 30 p. Illus.

Ludvigsen tells of the great Mercedes cars, the men who designed them and the men who drove them. Great victories and heart-breaking defeats are re-created for generations born too late to have seen them. It covers the 1900 Benz through the C111 Wankel. The book was awarded the Montagu Trophy for excellence in motoring history.

______. PORSCHE: EXCELLENCE WAS EXPECTED: THE COMPLETE HISTORY OF PORSCHE SPORTS AND RACING CARS. Automobile Quarterly Library Series. New York: E.P. Dutton and Co., 1977. 800 p. Illus., col. photos.

This is a complete history of Porsche from the early experimental years to the latest model 928. Ludvigsen had extensive cooperation from the Porsche family and spent twenty years assembling material. There are over 1,000 illustrations, both photographs and paintings, many in full color. This is a masterful work.

Pritchard, Anthony. COMPETITION CARS OF EUROPE. Indianapolis: Bobbs-Merrill Co., 1970. 208 p. Index. B/w photos.

Pritchard includes eighteen different competition cars, each of which played some role in the development of motor racing. Some, like Ferrari, Mercedes, Porsche, and Alfa Romeo, were usually successful. Others, like the CTA-Arsenal and the SEFAC, were failures.

Still others, like the Gordini and the Talbot, had ups and downs, but eventually faded away. The author is an expert and provides a wealth of technical data about each car.

_____. MASERATI: A HISTORY. New York: Arco Publishing Co., 1976. 399 p. Index. B/w photos.

The only full history of Maserati cars yet published, the book gives a comprehensive account of Maserati racing successes and failures, and describes the many different cars built by the company. Full specifications are given for each model along with detailed results for all works cars entered in Grand Prix, Voiturette, and sports cars events. The accounts of the racing seasons from 1926 to 1965 are brief but well done.

_____. PORSCHE. London: Pelham Books, 1969. 199 p.

Pritchard traces the evolution of the Porsche racing efforts from the early sports cars through its present successes in prototype and sports car racing. Porsche rally achievements are included as well as the story of its Le Mans effort. It is an interesting look at the Stuttgart firm.

Pulfer, Harry. MODEL T FORD IN SPEED AND SPORT. Arcadia, Calif.: Post Motor Books, 1956. 224 p. Illus.

Nostalgia runs high in motorsports and Pulfer returns to the days when the Model T was king of the dirt tracks. Names like Frontenac, Winfield, Chevrolet Brothers, Atwater Kents, Riley, Fronty-Ford, and others are present throughout. The speed secrets and ideas tried first on the Model T, by some very inventive minds, are detailed. This is probably the most authoritative and complete collection of speed and sport conversion information for the Model T.

Rusz, Joe. PORSCHE SPORT 1976/77. Seal Beach, Calif.: Ruszkiewicz Publishing, 1977. 104 p. Illus.

This is a chronicle of Porsche's road racing activities during 1975 coupled with a variety of articles on other Porsche-powered vehicles.

Sloniger, Jerry. PORSCHE: THE 4-CYLINDER, 4-CAM SPORTS AND RACING CARS. Newfoundland, N.J.: Haessner, 1977. 128 p.

An illustrated history of the Porsche 4-cylinder, 4-cam sports, and racing cars. Some of the models included are the 550 Spyder, the 500A/1500 RS, 718 RSK, Carreras, the Abarth Carrera GTL, and the 904 GTS. A chapter on engine development is also included.

Tanner, Hans. FERRARI. 4th ed., rev. New York: Drake Publishers, 1974.

350 p. Appendixes. Col. and b/w photos.

This comprises a standard work on the history of Ferrari and his competition efforts. Tanner is an expert on Ferrari having worked for Ferrari as a regular employee and racing team manager. This edition covers through 1973. Appendixes provide race results, driver statistics, technical specifications, and performance information.

_____. THE RACING FORDS. New York: Meredith Press, 1968. 305 p. Appendixes. Illus.

An illustrated history of the Ford car and engine in racing, it is not as dry as most works of this type tend to be. The chapters on Indianapolis and on GT's and prototypes are especially interesting. The appendixes list Ford racing records.

Twite, Michael; Taylor, Roger; and Windsor, David. PROTOTYPE 1968-70: A DETAILED ANALYSIS OF THE WORLD'S LEADING RACING CARS. London: Pelham Books, 1969. 95 p. Photos., drwgs.

PROTOTYPE is illustrated with photographs and drawings as well as detailed scale drawings of some of the world's finest racing cars. The scale drawings are particularly interesting and give the racing enthusiast an excellent view of the automobiles. Drawings were done by Roger Taylor and photographs by David Windsor.

Valkenburgh, Paul Van. CHEVROLET-RACING . . . ? FOURTEEN YEARS OF RAUCOUS SILENCE. Newfoundland, N.J.: Haessner, 1972. 320 p.

This book is the history of surreptitious racing activity at Chevrolet during the time the car manufacturer was officially out of racing competition (1959-70). The book contains much technical material about engines and suspensions and is not designed to appeal to the average race fan. Specific teams covered are Jim Hall and the famous Chaparral, Roger Penske and Mark Donohue, and the exploits of Smokey Yunick. The book's usefulness is hampered by the lack of an index.

Weitmann, Julius Joseph. PORSCHE STORY. 2d ed., rev. Translated from the German by Charles Meisl with additional material edited by Michael Kettlewell. London: Stephens, 1971. 288 p. Photos.

This is the competition history of Porsche. Each year has a separate chapter. Chapters on designing and building the cars are also included along with listings of production and competition cars and victories won through 1971.

Tracks

Bayley, Joseph. THE VINTAGE YEARS AT BROOKLANDS. Norwich, Engl.: Goose and Sons, 1968. 130 p.

Bayley allows a look at an epic era of auto racing through events held at the famous Brooklands race track in Great Britain.

Boddy, William. THE MOTOR SPORT BOOK OF DONINGTON. London: Grenville Publishing Co., 1973. 121 p. Illus.

Boddy has pulled together a collection of articles from MOTOR SPORT which deal with the Donington race track in Great Britain. It primarily deals with the years 1933 to 1939.

Carrick, Peter. SILVERSTONE: THE STORY OF BRITAIN'S FASTEST CIRCUIT. London: Pelham Books, 1974. 174 p. Index. Illus.

Silverstone was a wartime airfield which became one of the most famous motor racing circuits in the world. Emphasis is on the outstanding races, exciting events, world class and outstanding drivers, and other unique characters who have been a part of the Silverstone epic through 1973.

Keays, Pressly [R.]. THE GILMORE RECORD: 1934 THROUGH 1950. North Hollywood, Calif.: The author, n.d. 14 p. Paper-bound.

A unique contribution to motorsport literature, this is an outline presentation of all drivers with Gilmore feature race victories from 1934 through 1950 when the track ceased operations. The Gilmore track was located in Los Angeles. Bits of Gilmore racing information are interspersed with the lists. This booklet must be purchased directly from the author (see chapter 12).

Klemantaski, Louis, and Frostick, Michael. MOTOR RACING CIRCUITS OF EUROPE. New York: Macmillan Co., 1958. 96 p. B/w photos., maps.

Klemantaski and Frostick have produced a valuable addition to any racing collection. Thirteen European race tracks are described along with a circuit map of each track and photographs of competition on these tracks. Covered are Spa in Belgium; Le Mans, Montlhery, Reims, and Rouen in France; the Nurburgring in Germany; Aintree, Goodwood, Oulton Park, and Silverstone in England; Zandvoort in Holland; Monza in Italy; and Monte Carlo in Monaco.

Tommasi, Tommaso. FROM INDIANAPOLIS TO LE MANS. Introduction by Juan Manuel Fangio. Secaucus, N.J.: Derbibooks, 1974? 240 p. Col. and b/w photos. by David Phipps.

Ten of the world's leading circuits are discussed in detail in this large format book. An interesting feature of each section is a description of a lap around the track by a famous driver. An additional chapter describes all of the world's major road courses. The photographs, many of which are in color, are one of the book's strongest points.

Competition Instruction Manuals

Anderson, Dick. GETTING READY TO RACE: GUIDE TO COMPETITION DRIVERS' SCHOOLS. Rev. ed. New York: Sports Car Press, 1968. 124 p.

Anderson tells beginners how to prepare for racing: licensing requirements, driver schools, basic equipment needed, and some elementary car preparation. Some rules have been changed but much of the basic information is still valid. Some of the material was provided by Bill Stone.

Frere, Paul. SPORTS CAR AND COMPETITION DRIVING. Cambridge, Mass.: Robert Bentley, 1966. 144 p. Photos., diags.

This is a practical manual written for the car owner who wishes to become a better than average driver and for rallyists and club racers who want to go faster. Frere's book gives valuable instruction on a variety of techniques. He explains the correct lines on various corners, racing starts, braking points, slides and drifts, slipstreaming, and passing. Tips on race tactics, timekeeping, pit work, choosing tires and gear ratios, and learning a circuit make the book extremely useful. Frere was himself a Grand Prix driver, Le Mans winner, and an engineer.

Gardner, Frank, and Nye, Doug. CASTROL RACING DRIVERS' MANUAL. New York: Arco Publishing Co., 1974. 165 p. Photos., diags.

Frank Gardner has spent twenty-five years driving all types of racing cars and he has, with Doug Nye's assistance, set down something of what he has learned in those years. He talks about proper cornering techniques, ways to sort out handling problems, tires, getting a sponsor, and how to drive formula and sports racing machinery. This last chapter is particularly interesting since formula cars and sports racers are very different from production cars.

Hall, Wally. HOW TO START MOTOR RACING. New York: British Book Centre, 1973. 112 p.

A good book for would-be racers on how to get started in motor racing. Definite British slant, but it is still good for novices.

Holbert, R.; Holbert, Al; and Bochroch, Albert R. DRIVING TO WIN. Newfoundland, N.J.: Haessner, 1978. 195 p.

This is one of the most current and best instructional manuals related to driving techniques, race vehicle preparation, including detailed information regarding sponsorship acquisition by two of America's most successful race drivers as told to Al Bochroch. Al Holbert was selected to compete in the International Race of Champions.

Houlgate, Deke. "So You Want To Be a Race Driver." In THE HANDBOOK OF HIGH PERFORMANCE DRIVING, pp. 149-86. New York: Dodd, Mead and Co., 1975.

A very informative guide to the main types of automobile racing and the main sanctioning bodies. This type of material is dated very quickly and already the information on age and sex requirements for certain divisions has changed. However, there are enough basic rules for the aspiring race driver in these pages to make their reading an asset. Addresses are provided.

Jenkinson, Denis. THE RACING DRIVER; THE THEORY AND PRACTICE OF FAST DRIVING. Cambridge, Mass.: Robert Bentley, 1964. 207 p. Photos, diags.

One of the classics of motor racing literature, Jenkinson's descriptions of techniques of fast driving are must reading for the expert and novice alike. Jenkinson has been a passenger in cars driven by Stirling Moss, Juan Fangio, and Mike Hawthorn and gives a readable eyewitness account of driving at the limit. Jenkinson rode as passenger in four consecutive Mille Miglias, raced motorcycles, and has been a racing journalist for many years. His ability to describe what he has seen and done make this one of the standard works.

Johnson, Alan. DRIVING IN COMPETITION. 3d ed. Newport Beach, Calif.: Bond, Parkhurst Publications, 1976. 156 p.

This is a guide for the novice race driver attempting to enter sports car competition. This book covers what type of car to buy, what expenses to face, how to obtain a license, and some basic competition driving techniques. Although this is a recent edition, the license requirements given are not updated. Any novice must check with SCCA for proper licensing requirements.

O'Shea, Paul. A GUIDE TO COMPETITION DRIVING. Edited by Bern Williams. Modern Sports Car Series. New York: Sports Car Press, 1957. 126 p.

O'Shea explains techniques used by professional racers to compete and win. The primary emphasis is on cornering and the four-wheel drift.

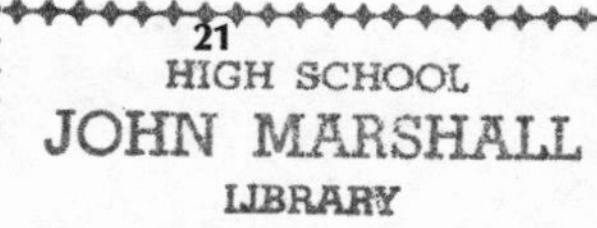

Auto Racing

Taruffi, Piero. THE TECHNIQUE OF MOTOR RACING. Translated from the Italian by D.B. Tubbs. Foreword by Juan Manuel Fangio. Cambridge, Mass.: Robert Bentley, 1958. 125 p. Photos., diags., maps.

One of the three classic works on competition driving, the book covers shifting, braking, cornering, tactics, physical training, and racing circuits. Although both cars and tracks have changed considerably through the years, Taruffi's book remains a standard work read by most would-be race drivers. The book contains maps of major circuits.

Turner, Stuart. THE WAY TO WIN: A COMPETITOR'S GUIDE TO SUCCESS IN MOTOR SPORTS. Croydon, Engl.: Motor Racing Publications, 1974. 176 p.

Turner provides much useful information on competition in international caliber events. Some topics covered are how to begin driving, codriving, car preparation, accessories for rallying, and additional information on racing. The information provided here can help people avoid common pitfalls and extra expenses in getting a program underway.

Motor Racing Safety

Cooper-Evans, Michael. RISK LIFE, RISK LIMB. London: Pelham Books, 1968. 128 p. Photos.

Cooper-Evans discusses thoughts and experiences relating to safety in that hazardous sport of speed.

Henderson, Michael. MOTOR RACING IN SAFETY: THE HUMAN FACTORS. London: Patrick Stephens, 1968. 167 p.

This offers valuable and not too often published material on the safety factors involved in auto racing. Besides covering the physiology and psychology of the race driver the book covers external factors (heat, cold, noise, vibrations) that affect a driver, protective clothing, fire prevention and extinction devices, and restraint systems. A good bibliography on motor racing is provided. A well-done scientifically approached work, this is a valuable addition to motor racing literature.

Jim Clark Foundation. GRAND PRIX ACCIDENT SURVEY, 1966-72. London: 1974. 64 p. Illus.

This study was done to help establish the apparent causes of 224 accidents in races or practice session during the years 1966-72. Data was acquired in part from eyewitness reports and expert analysis of the accidents. The foundation was established in memory of Grand Prix driver Jim Clark to contribute to safety in motor sport. Much useful information on driver and spectator safety, fire control, and car maintenance has resulted from this report.

_____. RESEARCH REPORT ON FIRE RESISTANT CLOTHING. London: 1973? 56 p.

This report is an excellent survey of test results of twenty-five different combinations of fire-protective clothing. A supplement covers experiments run during the winter of 1971-72 on ten fabrics. Four of these materials revealed significant improvement. The supplement must be used with the original report.

Kahn, Mark. THE DAY I DIED. New York: International Publishers Services, 1974. 145 p. Photos.

The emphasis is on crashes--what actually happens in the seconds before and during a crash. Some prominent drivers give their firsthand impressions of these frightening events. Some drivers contributing are Denis Hulme, Stirling Moss, Innes Ireland, motorcycle racer Mike Hailwood, and Jackie Stewart.

Biography

Abbott, Hans, ed. WHO'S WHO IN RACING. Tiffin, Ohio: The author, 1973? 64 p.

This is a pictorial directory of drivers competing at some of the smaller tracks in the Midwest as well as at the Indianapolis Motor Speedway. Information varies from brief biographical data to only a picture. There is no table of contents or index. There were to be other editions but the editors of this bibliography have been unable to locate them.

Bradley, W.F. ETTORE BUGATTI: A BIOGRAPHY. Abingdon, Engl.: Motor Racing Publications, 1948. 152 p.

Ettore Bugatti (Le Patron), motor manufacturer, specialist in racing cars, is synonymous with the early days of motor racing. His contributions to the sport and to the development of the automobile were immeasurable. Bradley wrote this biography in close collaboration with Bugatti's family and friends, and published it only a few months after Le Patron's death. The book deals not only with Bugatti race cars but the part Bugatti and his drivers played in the resistance to the German occupation in World War II.

Dillon, Mark. AMERICAN RACE CAR DRIVERS. Minneapolis, Minn.: Lerner Publications Co., 1974. 51 p. Index. Illus.

This is a fifth-grade level book that presents biographies of American racing drivers A.J. Foyt, Richard Petty, Parnelli Jones, and Mark Donohue.

Higdon, Hal. FINDING THE GROOVE. New York: G.P. Putnam's Sons, 1973. 312 p.

A collection of interviews with drivers from all areas of racing, these conversations are not intended to be an in-depth analysis but are pleasant reading for the racing fan. Drivers covered include Mario Andretti, Mark Donohue, Richard Petty, Sam Sessions, Bobby Allison, Al and Bobby Unser, Mike Hiss, Don Garlits, Jimmy Caruthers, George Follmer, Mike Mosley, and Peter Revson.

Jenkinson, Denis, and Posthumus, Cyril. VANWALL: THE STORY OF TONY VANDERVELL AND HIS RACING CARS. London: Patrick Stephens, 1975. 176 p. Photos.

The Vanwall car hit the road to success with a triumph at the British Grand Prix at Aintree in 1967. Jenkinson and Posthumus discuss the cars, Vandervell, and his team. An interesting book and a great success story.

Libby, Bill. GREAT AMERICAN RACE DRIVERS. New York: Cowles Book Co., 1970. 245 p. Index. B/w photos.

Over fifty drivers are represented in this historical array of racing talent. Championship, sports car, stock car, drag racer, and all facets of racing are covered. Separate chapters are devoted to A.J. Foyt and Richard Petty. Unique in this work is the final chapter, which is a series of records of most of the important drivers and races in the United States, as well as a smattering of those of the world. Some rankings of drivers are attempted.

______. SUPERDRIVERS: THREE AUTO RACING CHAMPIONS. Champaign, Ill.: Garrard Publishing Co., 1977. Illus.

Libby provides biographies of three champion drivers, two of whom are no longer active. The two retired drivers are two-time Indy winner Rodger Ward and Lee Petty, father of current stock car racing star Richard Petty. The third driver included is drag racer Don "Big Daddy" Garlits.

Nolan, William F. CARNIVAL OF SPEED: TRUE ADVENTURES IN MOTOR RACING. New York: G.P. Putnam's Sons, 1973. 191 p. Index.

Nolan presents brief essays on several memorable races and drivers. Included are Bill Vukovich, Sr., Nuvolari, Ted Horn, Earl Cooper, Ricardo Rodriguez, "Cannon Ball" Erwin Baker, and Phil Hill.

These essays were originally published in magazines.

Olney, Ross [R.]. AUTO RACING'S YOUNG LIONS. New York: G.P. Putnam's Sons, 1977. 127 p. Index. Illus.

The careers of seven sons of early auto racing greats are covered in this Olney effort. Those included are Bill Vukovich, Jr., Richard Petty, Duane "Pancho" Carter, Dannie Thompson, Gary Bettenhausen, Johnny Parsons, Buddy Baker, and their fathers. Each chapter is brief but interesting and informative.

______. MODERN AUTO RACING SUPERSTARS. New York: Dodd, Mead and Co., 1978. 112 p. Index. B/w photos.

Olney has written short career sketches of seven currently competing drivers from USAC, NASCAR, and the Formula I circuit. Drivers included are James Hunt, Mario Andretti, A.J. Foyt, Niki Lauda, Bobby Allison, and Al and Bobby Unser. The sketches are aimed at the younger reader.

______. SUPERSTARS OF AUTO RACING. New York: G.P. Putnam's Sons, 1975. 126 p. Index. B/w photos.

This book contains brief career sketches of eleven "super stars" in all fields of racing. A.J. Foyt, Gordon Johncock, and Roger McCluskey from USAC; Richard Petty from NASCAR; Mark Donohue, Peter Revson, and George Follmer from road racing; Jackie Stewart, Emerson Fittipaldi, and Jody Scheckter from Formula I; and Don Garlits from drag racing make up Olney's list. Too many errors, mundane prose, and lack of style make this book dull reading.

Orr, Frank. WORLD'S GREAT RACE DRIVERS. New York: Random House, 1972. 152 p. Index. B/w photos.

Short profiles of eleven great race drivers in all classes of the sport. Included are A.J. Foyt, Richard Petty, Jackie Stewart, Mario Andretti, Bruce McLaren, Don Garlits, Mark Donohue, Jimmy Clark, Parnelli Jones, and Bobby and Al Unser. This book is for young people as well as adults.

Porsche, Ferry, and Bentley, John. WE AT PORSCHE; THE AUTOBIOGRAPHY OF DR. ING, H.C. FERRY PORSCHE. New York: Doubleday and Co., 1976. 290 p.

This autobiography tells not only the story of Ferry Porsche but also Ferdinand Porsche and the Porsche firm. The time period spans the two world wars and includes some of the most famous racing machines ever built. It also tells the story of the "People's Car" known now as the Volkswagen. While racing is only part of the

Porsche story one cannot talk about racing without mentioning Porsche. The technical descriptions are fascinating and it is a well-written readable book.

Yates, Brock. RACERS AND DRIVERS: THE FASTEST MEN AND CARS FROM BARNEY OLDFIELD TO CRAIG BREEDLOVE. 2d ed., rev. and enl. Indianapolis: Bobbs-Merrill Co., 1976. 95 p. B/w photos.

A series of short two-to-three-page biographies of famous racing car and driver combinations, such as Ralph De Palma and the "Grey Ghost," Pete DePaolo and the Duesenberg, Duke Nalon and the Novi, A.J. Foyt and the Coyote, are presented. The biographies are more about the men than the cars. Grand Prix, Indianapolis type, stock and drag racing combinations are all included.

B. INDIANAPOLIS CARS (Championship Racing)

Andretti, Mario, with Collins, Bob. WHAT'S IT LIKE OUT THERE? Chicago: Henry Regnery, 1970. 282 p.

The biography of Indy 500 winner Mario Andretti, this book relates his relationship with his twin brother Aldo; his hard way up through the midgets and sprints; his relationships with many of the famous and near famous on the Indy Championship Trail including Don Branson, Clint Brawner, and A.J. Foyt; and his 1969 500 victory. This biography catches the true flavor of championship racing. It is an honest, unvarnished story.

Berger, Phil, and Bortstein, Larry. THE BOYS OF INDY. New York: Sterling Publishing Co., 1977. 181 p. Photos.

Twelve competitors in the Indianapolis 500 tell about their efforts, successes, and failures. The twelve are Wally Dallenbach, Mark Donohue, Al Unser, Salt Walther, Johnny Rutherford, Lloyd Ruby, Johnny Parsons, Jan Opperman, Jerry Karl, Bill Simpson, Dick Simon, and John Martin. A notable omission is four-time Indy winner A.J. Foyt. It is difficult to see how one can do a book on Indianapolis without comments or a discussion of Foyt. But the book is interesting and basically well done.

Bloemker, Al. 500 MILES TO GO: THE STORY OF THE INDIANAPOLIS SPEEDWAY. New York: Coward, McCann and Geoghegan, 1966. 315 p. Index. Appendix.

A well-done valuable historical presentation of the Indianapolis 500 written by the Indianapolis Speedway's public relations man. Bloemaker takes the reader on a fascinating trip through time starting with Carl Fisher's acquisition of the race plant and progressing to Harroun winning the first 500, De Palma, Rickenbacker, Shaw, Hulman, the Novis, Vukovich, USAC replacing AAA, Foyt, and ending in the era of the rear engine revolution. The book is packed with detail and includes an appendix which lists the top ten finishes in each race up to 1965, and prize money through 1965.

Brawner, Clint, and Scalzo, Joe. INDY 500 MECHANIC. Radnor, Pa.: Chilton Book Co., 1975. 194 p.

Brawner and Scalzo pull few punches in their behind-the-scenes tour of the Indianapolis 500. Brawner has had an impressive array of drivers including Bob Sweikert, Jimmy Bryan, A.J. Foyt, Eddie Sachs, and his 500 winner, Mario Andretti. He discusses them all. This is good reading for the average fan.

Calvin, Jean. THOSE INCREDIBLE INDY CARS. Modern Sports Car Series. New York: Sports Car Press, 1973. 126 p. Tables. B/w photos.

This entry in the modern sports car series starts out routinely covering the history of Indianapolis from its beginning to 1960 in mundane fashion. However the book hits its stride about half way through when the author devotes separate chapters to three modern racing teams--All American Racers, STP and their turbine, and Team McLaren. These chapters alone warrant the inclusion of the book in a racing collection. There are tables of the fast qualifiers and winners of the Indianapolis 500, Pocono 500, and Ontario 500 through 1972 but this information could be found more easily elsewhere.

Catlin, Russ. THE LIFE OF TED HORN, AMERICAN RACING CHAMPION. Los Angeles: Clymer Publishing, 1949. 223 p. Illus.

Although Ted Horn never won the Indianapolis 500, he achieved true greatness. AAA champion for three consecutive years, he was very successful everywhere else. This book is one of the classic works of auto racing biography.

Clymer, Floyd. INDIANAPOLIS 500 MILE RACE HISTORY. Los Angeles: Clymer Publishing, 1946. 320 p. Diags. Photos.

A classic work, this history reviews in detail every 500-mile race up to 1941 and the cessation of the race for the duration of World War II. Contains photographs, diagrams, and details not found anywhere else. The lack of an index hinders its use, but the chronological arrangement helps somewhat.

DePaolo, Peter. WALL SMACKER: THE SAGA OF THE SPEEDWAY. Pittsburgh, Pa.: DePaolo Publishing Co., 1935. 271 p. B/w photos.

A true classic, this autobiography recreates the early days of auto racing and the Rickenbacker era at the speedway. All the giants of the sport are part of DePaolo's story--De Palma, Duesenberg, Miller, Murphy, Milton, Petillo, and others. It was a colorful age and DePaolo tells it as only one who has been there can do.

Devaney, John, and Devaney, Barbara. THE INDIANAPOLIS 500: A COMPLETE PICTORIAL HISTORY. Chicago: Rand McNally and Co., 1976. 286 p. Index. Photos.

The Devaneys provide a narrative highlight of each race with background from qualifications and practice. Comments from competitors add color to their descriptions. The top ten finishers, their cars, and prize money as well as technical statistics for each are given. The book's strongest point are the three hundred or more photographs, many never published before. Jack Fox's "Indianapolis 500" is stronger on statistics.

Dolan, Edward F., and Lyttle, Richard B. JANET GUTHRIE: FIRST WOMAN DRIVER AT INDIANAPOLIS. Garden City, N.Y.: Doubleday and Co., 1978. 80 p. Index. Photos.

This is a brief biography of Janet Guthrie who made history in 1977 by becoming the first woman to qualify for the Indianapolis 500. The authors recount Janet's early interest in airplanes and her switch to sports car racing. The development of her racing career is covered; and the excitement of her attempts and final success in qualifications at the speedway is described. The book is written primarily for the younger race fan.

Dorson, Ron. THE INDY 500: AN AMERICAN INSTITUTION UNDER FIRE. Newport Beach, Calif.: Bond, Parkhurst Publications, 1974. 229 p.

Despite the book's title and its coverage of the ill-fated 1973 Indy 500 this book is actually pro racing. While the quotes and descriptions of the drivers are interesting the most valuable part of the book is the space devoted to men who do not race--the officials, the press, the mechanics, the 500 festival folk. Included are Joe Quinn, Tony Hulman, Harland Fengler, Pat Vidan, Donald Davidson, Grant King, and Sid Collins.

Engel, Lyle Kenyon. THE INCREDIBLE A.J. FOYT. 2d ed. New York: Arco Publishing Co., 1977. 160 p. Index. Photos.

Engel and the staff of AUTO RACING MAGAZINE have put together a history of A.J. Foyt's career from his early races in Houston to his Indianapolis wins. Foyt is a much publicized driver and many well-known stories about this legendary driver are included, but there is little insight into Foyt the man. This is more a career summary than a biography.

______. MARIO ANDRETTI: THE MAN WHO CAN WIN ANY KIND OF RACE. New York: Arco Publishing Co., 1970. 157 p. Appendix. B/w photos.

A fairly run-of-the-mill biography of Mario Andretti, 1969 Indianapolis winner, is presented. It covers Mario's career from its beginning in Trieste, Italy, to 1970. There is very little about Mario the man but all his major races and his many duels with A.J. Foyt and Bobby Unser are related. The appendix covers his career statistics to 1970.

______. 132 OF THE MOST UNUSUAL CARS THAT EVER RAN AT INDIANAPOLIS. New York: Arco Publishing Co., 1970. 159 p. Index Photos.

This is a collection of odd and not-so-odd cars which have competed or attempted to compete in the 500. Yunick's sidecar, the midengined Porsche, the turbines, and many early cars are included. The index is poor and information on each car is very brief. This book is primarily comprised of photographs.

______. THE INDIANAPOLIS "500": THE WORLD'S MOST EXCITING AUTO RACE. New York: Four Winds Press, 1970. 223 p. Appendix. B/w photos.

Produced by Engel and the editors of AUTO RACING MAGAZINE, this is pictorial coverage of the races up till 1969. One chapter covers 1911 to 1962; then individual chapters take the reader up to 1969. Some text provided. An appendix consists of charts for each race for 1911 to 1969 listing driver, car name, starting and finishing positions, qualifying speed, chassis, car number, type, and cylinders.

Fox, Jack C. THE ILLUSTRATED HISTORY OF THE INDIANAPOLIS 500. 2d ed. Speedway, Ind.: Carl Hungness Publishing, 1975. 327 p. Photos.

The most complete pictorial history of the Indianapolis 500 available today has been compiled by Fox. The lineup of each race complete with driver, car, and entrant is given from the first race in 1911 until 1975. Excellent driver performance records are included plus unique list of nonqualifiers from 1911 to date.

Gerber, Dan. INDY: THE WORLD'S FASTEST CARNIVAL RIDE. Englewood Cliffs, N.J.: Prentice-Hall, 1977. 82 p. Col. and b/w photos.

This is a rather inane and unoriginal book on the Indianapolis 500 by a writer who does not seem to like either the race or the city. His accounts of some interesting conversations with drivers and officials are good but the rest of the material is superficial and provincial.

Gilbert, John. AN INTERVIEW WITH BOBBY UNSER. Mankato, Minn.:

Creative Education, 1977. 31 p. Photos. by Vernon J. Biever.

A brief biography of two-time Indianapolis winner Bobby Unser, this book is aimed at younger readers.

Granatelli, Anthony [Andy]. THEY CALL ME MISTER 500. Chicago: Henry Regnery, 1969. 341 p.

In this entertaining, colorful autobiography of racing personality and winning 500 car owner Andy Granatelli, Granatelli spins tale after tale of his days of hot rod racing, his reign as a STP executive, the frustrating days of his legendary Novis, and the battles for his controversial turbo-cars. His reminiscences are star-studded with names such as Parnelli Jones, Joe Leonard, Jimmy Clark, Jim Hurtubise, and Bobby Unser. This is good reading for race fans.

Higdon, Hal. SUMMER OF TRIUMPH. New York: G.P. Putnam's Sons, 1977. 245 p.

This is a story of the life of racing star Jimmy Caruthers and his losing bout against cancer. But this book is not a tale of death but a tale of a vibrant man in love with living and his own life-style. An inspiring portrayal of courage, this book is excellent.

______. THIRTY DAYS IN MAY: THE INDY 500. New York: G.P. Putnam's Sons, 1971. 190 p. Index.

In diary form and beginning with one May, Higdon covers the events of each day leading up to the 1970 Indianapolis 500. Practice, qualifications, and the race itself are covered.

Jackson, Robert [B.]. CHAMPIONSHIP TRAIL: THE STORY OF INDIANAPOLIS RACING. New York: Henry Z. Walck, 1970. 72 p.

This book presents only a rudimentary look at the men and machines that make up the Indianapolis 500. There is one chapter devoted to a fairly complete report of the 1968 Indianapolis 500. This book would probably be of interest only to a novice or a very young race fan.

Kenyon, Mel, as told to Darnall, Bruce A., and Christopulos, Mike. BURNED TO LIFE. Foreword by A.J. Foyt. Harrison, Ark.: New Leaf Press, 1976. 128 p.

This is the autobiography of Mel Kenyon, four-time USAC Midget Champion and Indy 500 driver. Kenyon was severely burned at Langhorne, Pennsylvania, in 1965 in a championship race and won his last three Midget titles with a special glove and pin to replace the lost fingers on his left hand. As a result of his accident Kenyon has drawn close to God and this biography is a religious bioggraphy. But the biography is not "goody-goody," but an honest look at racing and one man's courage. The religion as a theme does not overshadow the racing. This book is written at an easy reading level.

Kleinfield, Sonny. A MONTH AT THE BRICKYARD: THE INCREDIBLE INDY 500. New York: Holt, Rinehart and Winston, 1977. 227 p.

Kleinfield follows the fortunes of driver Johnny Parsons, car owner Tassi Vatis, and the crew of car 93 during the month of May 1976. The author also introduces others who play major and minor roles in the great speed classic. He recounts the pressures, frustrations, successes, and failures that are an integral part of auto racing. He also gives a bird's eye view of what it takes to run the Indianapolis 500. This is one of the better books on this race.

Krishef, Robert K. THE INDIANAPOLIS 500. Minneapolis: Lerner Publications Co., 1974. 51 p.

Krishef has compiled a historical presentation of the famed Indianapolis Motor Speedway beginning with its construction in 1909. This illustrated fifth grade reading level format includes information about the speedway, the race itself, the rules, the drivers, and a description of a typical race and its aftermath.

Libby, Bill. ANDRETTI. New York: Grosset and Dunlap, 1970. 196 p. Index. B/w photos.

A better-than-average racing biography, this one has a little more depth than most. It tells us a little about Andretti the man as well as recounting his entire career from its beginning in Italy to his 1969 Indianapolis win. Libby catches some of the excitement and color of the sport.

_____. CHAMPIONS OF THE INDIANAPOLIS 500: THE MEN WHO HAVE WON MORE THAN ONCE. New York: Dodd, Mead and Co., 1976. 175 p.

Libby has written a bland series of chapters about nine of the ten men who have won the Indianapolis 500 more than once. These are not in-depth pieces but short collections of the known facts about each man's racing career--nothing new here. Drivers covered are Tommy Milton, Louis Meyer, Wilber Shaw, Mauri Rose, Bill Vukovich, Rodger Ward, A.J. Foyt, Al Unser, and Bobby Unser. Johnny Rutherford is not included.

_____. FOYT. New York: Hawthorn Books, 1974. 218 p. Index. Illus.

This is an unauthorized biography of Anthony Joseph Foyt, Jr., a four-time Indianapolis winner and six times the national champion. Considered one of the greatest drivers in history, Foyt's career spans contemporary Indianapolis history.

______. PARNELLI: A STORY OF AUTO RACING. New York: E.P. Dutton and Co., 1969. 307 p.

Libby has woven a penetrating biography that looks at both Parnelli Jones the racer and Parnelli Jones the man. But the book goes beyond Jones into USAC championship racing itself, especially the Indianapolis 500. Here the reader will find personal glimpses of A.J. Foyt, Jim Hurtubise, Tony Bettenhausen, Mario Andretti, Dan Gurney, and literally dozens of drivers, owners, and mechanics who made up Jones's world of speed. This is an excellent biography of a brave man. Hard to put down, it draws an accurate picture of Indy championship racing. Its only flaw is the lack of an index.

Norquest, C. Lee. THE FABULOUS NOVI STORY. Indianapolis: Norquest Enterprises, 1963. 74 p. B/w photos.

This is a small but valuable history of the spectacular Novi cars that captured the hearts of many fans at the Indianapolis 500. Every Indy race the Novi appeared in or attempted to appear in is covered from 1946 to 1963. Every detail the author could glean has been included. From 1964 to 1966 supplements were issued. From 1967 to date a supplement has been issued but title changes have occurred as the Novi disappeared from the racing scene. The supplements for 1966 included the "Lotus Ford Story," for 1967 "Turbocar Story," and from 1969 to date a 500 race history.

Olney, Ross [R.]. DAREDEVILS OF THE SPEEDWAY. New York: Grosset and Dunlap, 1966. 151 p.

This is a series of short (five to eight pages) biographies of some of the men who have raced in the Indianapolis 500. The value of this book lies not with the pages devoted to winners such as A.J. Foyt and Mario Andretti, about whom much has been written, but rather with the sections devoted to Bill Vukovich, Ed Elision, Eddie Sachs, and Bobby Marshman about whom little has been seen in hardback print.

Scalzo, Joe. THE UNBELIEVABLE UNSERS. Chicago: Henry Regnery, 1971. 307 p. Photos.

Bobby and Al Unser, both two-time Indianapolis 500 winners, are the current stars of the racing Unser clan but are by no means the only winners in the family. Older brothers Jerry and Louie also had their moments of glory before tragedy struck. Daddy Unser (Jerry, Sr.) and Uncle Louie engraved "UNSER" on Pike's Peak long before Bobby conquered it for the ninth time. Even "Mom" Unser became a legend before her death in 1975. Scalzo wrote the book with the assistance of the Unser family and it is excellent reading for racing buffs. The book includes a rundown on the Unser racing records.

Shaw, Wilbur. GENTLEMEN, START YOUR ENGINES. New York: Coward, McCann and Geoghegan, 1955. 302 p.

The autobiography of Wilbur Shaw is a fascinating look at one of America's great drivers, a three-time Indy winner and president of the speedway when he died in a plane crash. Shaw was an amazing man and his story loses no excitement in the telling. Race driver, executive, hero, innovator, and developer, Shaw wore many hats and wore them well. From his early childhood to the start of the 1952 Indy 500, Shaw's story makes excellent reading.

Tippette, Giles. THE BRAVE MEN. New York: Macmillan Co., 1972. 393 p.

Tippette attempts to capture the reasons that men are willing to run incredible risks in auto racing and rodeo riding. Roger McCluskey is the subject of the auto racing segments. The author successfully recreates the emotions and tensions involved in top-level racing.

Yates, Brock. FAMOUS INDIANAPOLIS CARS AND DRIVERS. New York: Harper and Row, 1960. 219 p. Index. Photos.

General biographical sketches are painted of some of the earlier drivers at the Indianapolis 500. Among those covered are Ray Harroun, Ralph De Palma, Jimmy Murphy, Dave Lewis, Billy Arnold, Joel Thorne, Floyd Roberts, Wilbur Shaw, Fred Agabashian, and Bill Vukovich. No personal interview material is present.

_____. THE INDIANAPOLIS 500: THE STORY OF THE MOTOR SPEEDWAY. Revised "Golden Anniversary" edition. New York: Harper and Row, 1961. 182 p. Index. Illus.

Yates has compiled a historical account of the exciting Indianapolis 500 up to 1960 told in simple terms. Many well-known names appear in the text. An appendix lists the winners from 1911 to 1960 along with their car name, car make, engine make, cylinders, displacement, and average speed. There is nothing here that can't be found elsewhere, but the text is easy to absorb.

C. FORMULA I (Grand Prix Racing)

General

Bira Birabongse Bhanudej, Prince of Thailand. BITS AND PIECES. Yeovil,

Engl.: G.T. Foulis, 1950. 192 p. Photos.

Another of the classic works, Prince Bira's reminiscences bring to life a glorious and colorful era of auto racing--an age when many drivers were members of the aristocracy and an entirely different attitude was evident. This is a piece of motorsport history not to be missed.

Chula Chakrabongse, Prince of Thailand. ROAD RACING, 1936. Yeovil, Engl.: G.T. Foulis, 1972. 176 p. Photos.

Recently reissued, this classic work tells the story of the 1936 road racing season by one who was there. An epic era, it was the age of the massive Auto Unions and Mercedes that is not likely to come again. Prince Chula tells the story of the cars, events, and men who were a part of it.

Daley, Robert. CARS AT SPEED: THE GRAND PRIX CIRCUIT. Philadelphia: J.B. Lippincott, 1961. 303 p. Index.

This is a book about the track, the cars, and the men associated with major sports car racing. Many of the chapters are written around a major racing arena, and the races and men who have made it famous. Daley covers the Mille Miglia, Monte Carlo, Targa Florio, Zandvoort, Andennes Forest of Belgium, Le Mans, Silverstone, and the Nurburgring. The book contains much useful information of historical interest.

_____. THE CRUEL SPORT. New York: Bonanza Books, 1963. 220 p. B/w photos.

This is an excellent book on Grand Prix racing. The text is aided by black-and-white photos which transcend the passage of time. The text is good but the photography is superb--showing without sham the pressure and pain of driving the circuit. Daley has not attempted to cover all drivers and factories (Ferrari and Cooper are featured) but lets a few represent the many. The last half of the book pictorially displays practice and actual race competition.

Frewin, Michael, ed. THE INTERNATIONAL GRAND PRIX BOOK OF MOTOR RACING. New York: Doubleday and Co., 1965. 304 p.

This is an excellent anthology covering a broad spectrum of famous drivers and famous races. Included among the many are Stirling Moss, the Indianapolis 500, Jim Clark, Juan Fangio, Monza, Richard Seaman, and Tazio Nuvolari. Some interesting essays on the philosophy of racing are included.

Garrett, Richard. FAST AND FURIOUS: THE STORY OF THE WORLD CHAM-

PIONSHIP OF DRIVERS. Foreword by Graham Hill. New York: Arco Publishing Co., 1968. 205 p.

While this book does have a brief history of Grand Prix racing, it is actually the story of the 1967 Grand Prix season. It is the story of the tracks, the men, and the machines. This is an interesting and well-done book with a few photos and an index.

Harding, Anthony. HISTORIC RACING CARS TO 1939 IN COLOR. New York: Hippocrene Books, 1975. 63 p. Col. and b/w photo.

This is a thin volume devoting two pages each to representative types of Grand Prix cars from the Type Z Mors of 1902 to the Grand Prix Auto Union of 1938. A seven-page introduction by Harding provides a written history of the racing cars as a whole. The plates follow which include a brief written report on each car. Good for historical reference questions, this book is a worthy addition to the literature.

Hayward, Elizabeth. GRAND PRIX: THE COMPLETE BOOK OF FORMULA I RACING. New York: Dodd, Mead and Co., 1971. 179 p. Index. Diags. B/w photos.

Produced by Lyle Kenyon Engel and the editors of AUTO RACING MAGAZINE, this book captures the color, drama, and tragedy of Grand Prix racing. Concentrating on the thirteen major events run each year, Haywood has confined her work to cars and drivers of the 60s and early 70s. Sponsors, promoters, organizers, and the women in racing are also covered.

Hirst, Stephen. GRAND PRIX CHRONOLOGY (1950-71). New York: International Publishers Services, 1973. 240 p.

This chronology covers the history of Grand Prix racing from 1950-1971. Some of the great events were run and some of the greatest drivers in history competed during this era. Hirst has prepared a handy history of the period.

Hough, Richard. RACING CARS. London: Paul Hamlyn, 1966. 152 p.

Hough has compiled a history of racing covering careers of top drivers like Moss, Fangio, Nuvolari, and Shaw and memorable races at tracks like Silverstone, Brands Hatch, the Nuburgring, and Indianapolis.

Jackson, Robert B. SWIFT SPORT: CAR RACING UP CLOSE. New York: Henry Z. Walck, 1978. 54 p. B/w photos.

This brief book, aimed at the younger race fan, is composed primarily of black and white photographs. It deals exclusively with Grand Prix racing. Each photograph is carefully captioned and presents a close-up view of most aspects of Grand Prix racing.

Jenkinson, Denis. A STORY OF FORMULA ONE, 1954-60. London: Grenville Publishing Co., 1960. 159 p. Photos.

Jenkinson is one of the most knowledgeable and experienced automotive writers in the world. His experience and craftsmanship show in this brief discussion of the years from 1954 to 1960 in Formula I competition. He writes of the cars, drivers, and events with ease of long familiarity.

McCollister, John. ROAR IN THE CITY. Costa Mesa, Calif.: Performance Marketing, Inc., 1978. 64 p. Photos.

This is a pictorial essay on the running of the first Long Beach Grand Prix. The book is 8-1/2 by 11 inches and has more than half its photographs in color.

Miller, Peter. ACES WILD: THE STORY OF THE BRITISH GRAND PRIX. London: Pelham Books, 1972. 160 p.

Miller presents a history of the British Grand Prix skillfully interwoven with the history of the World Driving Championship as a whole. The book moves forward (a chapter devoted to each year) from the first British Grand Prix held at Silverstone in 1948 though races at Silverstone, Brands Hatch, and Aintree. It finishes up with the 1971 race also driven at Silverstone. A preview chapter on 1972 contains brief biographies. The material is by necessity condensed making this more a reference tool than a pleasure book.

Nye, Doug. THE BRITISH GRAND PRIX, 1926-76. London: Batsford, 1977. 144 p.

Nye, Doug, and Goddard, Geoffrey. THE CLASSIC SINGLE SEATERS: GREAT RACING CARS OF THE DONINGTON COLLECTION. Basingstoke, Engl.: Macmillan and Co., 1975. 143 p. Index. Col. illus.

Using the Donington Collection of single-seat racing cars, the author provides detailed profiles of the great personalities, places, races, marques, technical data, and racing records. He covers eighty exciting years of Grand Prix racing. It is a large format book and lavishly illustrated.

Posthumus, Cyril. CLASSIC RACING CARS. New York: Rand McNally and Co., 1977. 160 p. Drwgs.

For annotation, see p. 10.

Pritchard, Anthony. GRAND PRIX CARS OF THE 3-LITRE FORMULA. New York: Arco Publishing Co., 1977. 129 p. Photos.

Pritchard discusses the development and racing performance of each of the many cars designed to comply with the three-litre formula. The book is supplemented by details of the specifications of every significant car.

______. HISTORIC MOTOR RACING. New York: Grosset and Dunlap, 1969. 120 p. Col. and b/w photos.

The story of the development of Formula motor racing from the beginning until 1960 unfolds before the reader's eyes. This is more a story of machines than men. It is the tale of the Alfa Romeo, the Bugatti, the Mercedes-Benz, the Ferrari, and the Duesenberg.

Rosinski, Jose. FORMULA I RACING: THE MODERN ERA. New York: Grosset and Dunlap, 1974. 243 p. Col. and b/w photos.

The book begins with the technical revolution in 1959-60 and ends with the retirement of Jackie Stewart. It details the most important races of the era and discusses the drivers and the cars they drove. It lists winners of Grand Prix events counting toward the Drivers World Championship and results of the championship from 1959 to 1973.

Seidler, Edouard. CHAMPION OF THE WORLD; HOW JACKIE STEWART, MATRA AND RACING BLUE MADE IT TO THE TOP. Newfoundland, N.J.: Haessner, 1970. 108 p. Col. and b/w photos.

This is the story of Jackie Stewart's championship run in a French-built Matra. The prose is interesting and readable, but the photographs are the book's main beauty. They truly capture Grand Prix racing in all its glory and heartbreak. The book was originally published by AUTOMOBILE YEAR in Lausanne, Switzerland, but is distributed in the United States by Haessner.

Setright, L.J.K. THE GRAND PRIX: 1906-1972. New York: W.W. Norton, 1973. 320 p. Index. Col. and b/w photos.

A chronological history not of the men and tracks that make up Grand Prix racing but rather of the machinery that has made racing possible, this book is divided into 7 chapters each outlining a specific era of racing cars--1906-1911, 1912-1921, 1922-1933, 1934-1953, 1954-1960, 1961-1967, and 1968-1972. It is well written with good detail. Much research went into this book.

______. THE GRAND PRIX CAR, 1954-1966. New York: W.W. Norton, 1968. 422 p. Illus., col. and b/w photos.

Three parts make up this in-depth work on the Grant Prix car. The first covers the overall development of the car as well as the changes in the formula and the rules. The second part discusses the individual parts of the machine under the general categories of engine, chassis, suspension, tires, brakes, and aerodynamics. Considerable detail is given. Part 3 is entitled "Analysis and Synthesis." Twenty models of Grand Prix cars are presented in table form. The tables provide specifications on engines, transmission, chassis, and performance factors. Six of the models are discussed in detail. There is excellent coverage of GP cars of the period from 1954 to 1966.

Simon, Ted. GRAND PRIX YEAR. New York: Coward, McCann and Geoghegan, 1971. 280 p. Index. Appendixes.

This is a close look at Grand Prix racing--the drivers, machines, tracks, mechanics, and wives--focused on the 1970 racing season and the newly established March team. Simon takes the reader race by race through the agonies of a new team on the circuit giving personal glimpses of stars such as Chris Amon, Graham Hill, Jackie Stewart, and Mario Andretti. It is very well done. The first appendix is an analysis of points won in the 1970 world championship. The second appendix is a table of Grand Prix starting grids for 1970.

Taylor, Rich. FORMULA ONE: THE ULTIMATE IN RACING CARS. Golden Wheels Book. New York: Golden Press, 1974. 46 p. Col. and b/w photos.

The book begins with a very brief history of Formula I racing to 1974. A clear color diagram of a typical Formula I car gives an idea of the complexity of these cars. Recent models of eleven different marques are discussed and basic technical information is given. Color photographs by Bill Oursler accompany each description. There is no index.

Thompson, John. FORMULA ONE RECORD BOOK. London: Frewin, 1974. 240 p. Illus.

Thompson has gathered together data on all Formula I motor events from 1961 to 1965. This comprises an illustrated and detailed analysis of the races in this period. An unusual book with much valuable information, it has a large format.

Marques

Barnes, John W. FERRARI: TWENTY-FIVE YEARS OF FORMULA I. Introduction by Karl [E.] Ludvigsen. Newfoundland, N.J.: Haessner, 1975. 61 p. Drwgs.

Barnes covers the Ferrari Formula I cars from 1948 to 1974. There are twenty-five full-page beautifully detailed ink drawings accompanied by information and commentary on each car. Barnes is an excellent artist and the quality of his work is evident here.

Blundsden, John, and Phipps, David. THE STORY OF THE FORD GRAND PRIX ENGINE: ITS DESIGN AND DEVELOPMENT. Cambridge, Mass.: Robert Bentley, 1971. 224 p. Appendixes.

The design, development, and racing successes of this powerful engine are covered. The authors relate the background of the engine and Jimmy Clark's success with it up to the 1970 season. Appendixes list the Ford DFV and DFW engines built to May 1971 and the World Championship score sheet for the years 1966 to 1970. It was published in England under the title SUCH SWEET THUNDER: THE STORY OF THE FORD GRAND PRIX ENGINE.

Conway, Hugh Graham. GRAND PRIX BUGATTI. Cambridge, Mass.: Robert Bentley, 1968. 224 p. Illus.

Conway discusses the racing Bugatti types 35, 37, 43, and 51 and notes their successes and failures. Conway is considered an authority on the Bugatti automobile, and as a result this is an excellent book.

Hodges, David. THE LOTUS 49. London: Lionel Leventhal, 1970. 80 p. Appendixes. Photos.

A detailed discussion of one of racing's most notable and innovative cars, the Lotus 49 has been produced by Hodges who covers the developmental history of the car and provides several interesting appendixes which give a complete record of chassis numbers with changes of ownership of individual cars. It lists full race results with the cars raced, the drivers, and finishing positions.

Jenkinson, Denis. THE MASERATI 250F: A CLASSIC GRAND PRIX CAR. Foreword by Stirling Moss. New York: Arco Publishing Co., 1975. 80 p. Col. photos.

A complete record of the Maserati 250F, a very successful model with forty major wins to its credit between 1954 and 1957, is presented here. The book contains driver profiles, technical specifications, and a complete racing record. This is an excellent work on this exciting car.

______. MERCEDES-BENZ TYPE W125: GRAND PRIX 1937. London: Lionel Leventhal, 1970. 75 p. Drwgs., photos.

The Mercedes W125 is generally agreed to be one of the most powerful Grand Prix cars ever built and Jenkinson tells the story of how the car came into being. He discusses the developmental and design work, the car's competition record, and the technical specifications. He talks about the men who drove the W125-Caracciola, von Brauchitsch, Lang, Seaman, and Kautz as well as the legendary Mercedes manager, Alfred Neubauer.

Nye, Doug. GRAND PRIX TYRELLS, THE JACKIE STEWART CARS, 1970-1973. London: Macmillan and Co., 1975. 80 p. Index. Illus.

Here are all the highly successful Tyrells which carried Jackie Stewart to the world driving title. The book covers the years 1970 to 1973.

______. LOTUS: '61-'71: DESIGN REVOLUTION. Cambridge, Mass.: Robert Bentley, 1972. 288 p. Index. Appendixes.

This is a companion volume to Ian Smith's THE STORY OF LOTUS 1947-1960: BIRTH OF A LEGEND. Nye carries the Lotus legend onward into the eleven years during which Lotus cars and drivers won World Championships on four occasions. Each chapter is devoted to a year and is divided into three sections. The first section covers Lotus development during the year, the second covers major competition in which Lotus participated, and the third Lotus competition in lesser motoring events. The study is well done and full of information. It is an important addition to the literature.

Pritchard, Anthony. BRITISH RACING GREEN. London: Allen and Unwin, 1969. 294 p. Indexes. Appendix. Photos.

Pritchard covers the successes and failures of both small and large British racing teams in the post World War II years through the 1960s. Connaught, Vanwall, Cooper, Lotus, Jaguar, BRM, Lola, and others are included as well as information about non-British marques.

______. GRAND PRIX FERRARI. New York: W.W. Norton, 1974. 382 p. Index. Illus.

The book concentrates on the Ferrari Grand Prix cars, omitting sports cars, and prototypes. Each race in which a works Ferrari participated is mentioned and the major ones are analyzed. Technical developments and descriptions of the cars provide much information. Race results are listed.

Sheldon, Paul. MILESTONES BEHIND THE MARQUES. Newton Abbot, Engl.: David and Charles, 1976. 128 p. Index. Illus.

This book contains in-depth studies of the history of one model from ten world famous manufacturers. Each car is followed through its Formula I racing life. Manufacturers represented are BRM,

Cooper, Eagle, Ferrari, Honda, March, Matra, Repco-Brabham, Shadow, and Surtees. Each chapter begins with the physical specifications of the car covered followed by a history of several pages, then a chart showing all racing results. The book is a worthy addition to any racing collection.

Smith, Ian H. THE STORY OF LOTUS: 1947-1960 BIRTH OF A LEGEND. Cambridge, Mass.: Robert Bentley, 1970. 192 p. Illus.

Smith traces Colin Chapman and the Lotus automobile from the birth of the marque through the development and growth period to the emergence of the car into a successful Grand Prix contender. Doug Nye's companion volume covers the later years, while this one concentrates on the early developmental stages.

Thompson, Jonathan. THE FERRARI FORMULA I CARS 1948-1976. Tucson, Ariz.: Aztec Corp., 1976. 192 p. Drwgs., b/w photos.

Thompson provides complete photographic coverage of all Ferrari Formula I cars as well as some Formula II models and special project cars. Each chapter is devoted to the cars that used a particular engine. Each chapter gives a summary of technical specifications and a few line drawings followed by several pages of black-and-white photographs of the individual cars. Fairly detailed captions explain the significance of the variations. There is no index.

Biography

Bentley, John. THE DEVIL BEHIND THEM. Englewood Cliffs, N.J.: Prentice-Hall, 1958. 249 p.

This is an excellent collection of biographies of nine of the greatest race drivers of days past. Drivers covered are Wilbur Shaw, Achille Varzi, Stirling Moss, Tazio Nuvolari, Alberto Ascari, Richard Seaman, Raymond Sommer, Rudolf Caracciola, and Juan Fangio.

Birkin, Henry R.S. FULL THROTTLE. 1932. Reprint. London: G.T. Foulis, 1972. 291 p.

An autobiography, "Tim" as Birkin was more usually known to his peers, describes his career and with it a piece of an age. This book is one of several classic biographies which belong in any listing of motorsports titles as they deal with a particularly interesting and fruitful period of European racing.

Brabham, Jack, with Hayward, Elizabeth. WHEN THE FLAG DROPS. New York: Coward, McCann and Geoghegan, 1971. 240 p.

Fans will enjoy this well done autobiography of world champion race driver and car builder Jack Brabham. There is an interesting chapter on his childhood in Australia and a vivid word picture of his days at the Indianapolis 500. The rest is a tale of his struggles to rise to be one of the leading drivers on the Grand Prix circuit.

Caracciola, Rudolf. A RACING CAR DRIVER'S WORLD. New York: Farrar, Straus and Giroux, 1961. 232 p.

Rudolf Caracciola was one of the greatest of the European racing champions. In his autobiography the reader finds an intensely dedicated man who was totally committed to racing. Most of his career was spent in a Mercedes and his story is also Mercedes's story. When Rudi died in 1959, racing lost a giant. This is a fascinating and readable autobiography, which contains an epilogue by Allan Zone of Daimler-Benz and a chronological record of his races.

Chula Chakrabongse, Prince of Thailand. DICK SEAMAN, RACING CHAMPION. Yeovil, Engl.: G.T. Foulis, 1941.

One of the classic biographies of an early Grand Prix star, British driver Seaman is described by his princely competitor. This book helps recreate an age in motorsport that has vanished but remains fascinating.

Clark, Jim. JIM CLARK AT THE WHEEL: THE WORLD MOTOR RACING CHAMPION'S OWN STORY. New York: Coward, McCann and Geoghegan, 1964. 210 p. Appendix.

Clark wrote an autobiography that runs through 1964. A few pages are devoted to his childhood but the rest of the book focuses on his racing career. There is little here of Clark the man. The book is easily read with amusing anecdotes. There is a chapter on his racing in America including stories about Indianapolis and about his brush with stock car racing. An appendix contains a statistical record of Clark's achievements including a competition record, and a list of special awards and championships.

Cooper, John, with Bentley, John. THE GRAND PRIX CARPETBAGGERS: THE AUTOBIOGRAPHY OF JOHN COOPER. Garden City, N.Y.: Doubleday and Co., 1977. 230 p. Index. Appendix. Photos.

This is a very readable account of John Cooper's adventures in the world of motorsport. Cooper, one of the most innovative of the great designer-constructors has described the cars he built, the men who drove them, and some of the great events his cars won or lost. He takes the reader behind the scenes to the parties and politicking that are a part of racing. His coauthor, John Bentley, has much expertise in racing also, and the collaboration has resulted in an informative and entertaining book. Cooper's memory is a little hazy about procedures at Indianapolis but his version of Indy's first rear-engine machine is enlightening nonetheless. An appendix details the evolution of the Cooper.

Deschenaux, Jacques. JO SIFFERT. London: William Kimber, 1972. 208 p.

A biography of the racing career of the Swiss Grand Prix driver, Jo Siffert, the book covers the period from Siffert's beginnings as a motorcycle racer to the tragic day in 1971 when he was killed at Brands Hatch. This biography also contains a great deal of material on Rob Walker--the English car owner.

Dillon, Mark, and Haigh, Frank. INTERNATIONAL RACE CAR DRIVERS. Minneapolis: Lerner Publications Co., 1974. 51 p. Illus.

This is a fifth-grade reading-level publication that relates the careers of race drivers Dan Gurney, Mario Andretti, Jackie Stewart, and Emerson Fittipaldi.

Engel, Lyle Kenyon. JACKIE STEWART: WORLD DRIVING CHAMPION. New York: Arco Publishing Co., 1970. 159 p. B/w photos.

The text for this book was done by Elizabeth Hayward, who has a great knowledge of and feel for Grand Prix racing and its competitors. She recounts Stewart's career from the early club races in Scotland to the top of the Grand Prix world. She also acquaints the reader with Stewart the man in much fuller detail than is usual in this type of biography. The book contains a career summary. A chapter done with Helen Stewart, Jackie's wife, brings an extra dimension to the work.

THE EXCITING WORLD OF JACKIE STEWART. Cleveland: Collins-World, 1974. 88 p. Col. and b/w photos.

Here is a collection of impressions of former world champion Jackie Stewart given by an interesting variety of people. Contributors include Alistair MacLean, Eric Dymock, Ken Tyrell, Graham Gauld, and Sean Connery as well as Stewart himself. Each relates how he sees Stewart as a man and/or driver.

Fangio, Juan Manual. FANGIO. In collaboration with Marcello Giambertone. N.p.: Trust Books, 1963. 222 p.

No racing fan should miss Fangio's autobiography from his early childhood in Argentina through his 1951 World Championship season. It's an interesting look at a great champion and one of the classic biographical works. It was also published in 1961 by Temple Press under the title MY TWENTY YEARS OF RACING.

Fittipaldi, Emerson, and Hayward, Elizabeth. FLYING ON THE GROUND. London: William Kimber, 1973. 256 p.

Fittipaldi and Hayward have collaborated for an excellent biography of world driving champion Emerson Fittipaldi. Filled with quotes, it covers the bad and good times of his racing career but goes further to probe the life of the man behind the driver. The reading is fascinating.

Gauld, Graham. JIM CLARK REMEMBERED. New York: Arco Publishing Co., 1976. 143 p. Photos.

Gauld provides an objective look at the life of Grand Prix driver Jim Clark. The book contains many photographs--both racing and nonracing shots. It does not include one of Clark's fatal accident.

______, ed. JIM CLARK: PORTRAIT OF A GREAT DRIVER. New York: Arco Publishing Co., 1968. 204 p. Appendix.

This is a collection of views on Jim Clark written by the people who know him--authors include Graham Hill, Jackie Stewart, John Surtees, and Colin Chapman. An appendix details Clark's entire competition record.

Gill, Barrie, ed. MOTOR RACING: THE GRAND PRIX GREATS. New York: Drake Publishers, 1972. 166 p. Index. B/w photos.

After a brief introductory chapter on the characterization of Grand Prix drivers, Gill settles down to presenting biographies of ten of the most outstanding drivers of the circuit--Graham Hill, Stirling Moss, Jochen Rindt, Juan Fangio, Denny Hulme, Mike Hawthorn, Jim Clark, Jack Braham, Bruce McLaren, and Jackie Stewart. Most of the biographies are well done with interesting character sketches. A preface contains a balloting of England's motorsport drivers as to the greatest Grand Prix driver ever.

Halle, Jean-Claude. FRANCOIS CEVERT: A CONTRACT WITH DEATH. Translated by Denise and Michael Frostick. London: William Kimber, 1974. 213 p. B/w photos.

Francois Cevert was a man in love with life and racing but he did not expect to grow old. His biography pulsates with the spirit that was Cevert and the racing men who were his friends. When Cevert died Jackie Stewart withdrew from what was to be his last race. The love and pain of Stewart are apparent here.

There are many pages of quotes from Cevert. This is an excellent biography. There is no index.

Hawthorn, Mike. CHALLENGE ME THE RACE. London: W. Kimber, 1973. 240 p. Photos.

This autobiography is one of the classic books on motorsport. Hawthorn relates the story of his youth and his racing experiences from 1951 to 1957. Every race in this time span is discussed and makes fascinating reading.

Heglar, Mary Schnall. THE GRAND PRIX CHAMPIONS. Newport Beach, Calif.: Bond, Parkhurst Publications, 1973. 240 p.

Heglar has written a series of fairly short biographies of the thirteen men who had won the World Championship in Formula I cars from its beginning in 1950 through 1972. Especially helpful may be the sections on Nino Farina, Mike Hawthorn, John Surtees, Denny Hulme, and Jochen Rindt. A statistical section at the end of the book has historical information on every year of the championship from 1950 through a partially completed 1973.

Henry, Alan. RONNIE PETERSON; GRAND PRIX RACING DRIVER. Minneapolis: Motorbooks International, 1977. 160 p. Illus.

Written in association with Ronnie Peterson, Henry recounts Peterson's career through kart racing, Formula 3 and his triumph at Monaco, to Formula I and the beginning of the 1975 Grand Prix season. Peterson was always competitive and his biography is interesting reading.

Hill, Graham. LIFE AT THE LIMIT. 1st American edition. New York: Coward, McCann, and Geoghegan, 1970. 255 p.

Graham Hill chronicles the high points of his career emphasizing the years from 1958 to 1969.

Hill, Graham, with Ewart, Neil. GRAHAM. New York: St. Martin's Press, 1977. 175 p. Photos.

This is an excellent autobiography of Graham Hill allowing the reader to reach behind Hill the racer into the world of Hill the man. It also paints a picture of young talented driver Tony Brise who died in the plane crash with Graham. Since the book was nearly completed at Hill's death, his wife Bette has written a warm final chapter. This makes excellent reading.

Hodges, David, ed. GREAT RACING DRIVERS. New York: Arco Publishing Co., 1966. 176 p. B/w photos.

This is a well done book presenting the profiles of twenty-eight leading drivers who died or retired before 1966. Six to eight pages with photos cover each driver ending with a chart of their principal racing successes. The names stir the memory beginning with Camille Jenatzy, Caracciola, Nuvolari, Ascari, Seaman, Fangio, Hawthorn, and Collins. It is worthy to be part of any racing collection.

Hunt, James; Young, Eoin; and Hodges, David. JAMES HUNT AGAINST ALL ODDS. New York: E.P. Dutton and Co., 1977. 176 p.

James Hunt's own story of how he won the 1976 world driver's championship, this book covers his entire racing career and his association with the Hesketh racing team.

Jackson, Robert [B.]. ROAD RACERS: TODAY'S EXCITING DRIVING STARS. New York: Henry Z. Walck, 1977. 56 p. Photos.

This book may be small but it is packed full of information. Twenty-three famous road racers are profiled--including many drivers not found in other sources. Woman driver Lella Lombardi is included as well as John Watson, James Hunt, Patrick Depailler, Peter Gregg, Brett Lunger, and Jacques Laffite.

Jenkinson, Denis, ed. FANGIO. New York: W.W. Norton, 1973. 144 p. Photos.

Filmdon has aided in this pictorial odyssey through the career of Juan Manuel Fangio which is based on the documentary FANGIO and Fangio's personal recollections.

Lang, Hermann. GRAND PRIX DRIVER. Translated from the German by Charles Meisl. London: G.T. Foulis, 1953. 143 p. Illus.

Hermann Lang was one of Germany's greatest drivers and this is one of the classic autobiographies of the epic era of Grand Prix racing.

Lauda, Niki. THE ART AND SCIENCE OF GRAND PRIX DRIVING. Translated by David Irving. Osceola, Wis.: Motorbooks International, 1977. 245 p. Col. and b/w photos.

This is a comprehensive book containing the technicalities of Grand Prix driving along with the story of Niki Lauda's racing career. This book takes the reader on an exciting journey into a fast and furious world that covers Lauda's terrible crash at the Nurburgring, his postaccident emotions and his analysis and explanation of the theories and functions of the technical aspects of his Grand Prix car. Lauda describes racing techniques in general terms as well as relating how he feels about driving and what he feels are the ten toughest turns in Grand Prix racing.

______. MY YEARS WITH FERRARI. Osceola, Wis.: Motorbooks International, 1978. 237 p. Col. and b/w photos.

This book is a readable and articulate account of Lauda's career and his championship years. It provides a glimpse of his personal life and his attitudes towards racing and the people with whom he must deal. His account of his relationship with the legendary Enzo Ferrari gives a look behind the scenes at the activity of the Maranello factory which is rarely afforded outsiders. This is one of the better racing autobiographies. It was published in England under the title FOR THE RECORD.

Lurani, Giovani, in collaboration with Luigi Marinatto. NUVOLARI. Translated by John Eason Gibson. New York: William Morrow and Co., 1959. 223 p. Index. Appendix. Photos.

Tazio Nuvolari was one of the greatest drivers of his or any age and Count Lurani relates his triumphs, giving us vivid eyewitness accounts of some of the great races of the 1930s. Other famous drivers of the period, Varzi, Ascari, Campari, Rosemeyer, and others make this an interesting and valuable biography. It is indexed and illustrated with photographs. An appendix lists year, date, circuit, finishing position, and car make for Nuvolari's major races.

Manso, Peter. VROOOM!! CONVERSATIONS WITH THE GRAND PRIX CHAMPIONS. New York: Funk and Wagnalls, 1969. 227 p.

Manso presents a fascinating series of interviews with top Grand Prix drivers (several now dead) on a variety of subjects moving from how they feel about the dangers involved in racing to their motivation for racing, their relationships with their families, and their views on politics. The questions asked are a bit more probing than those usually found in published interviews making this recommended reading for all fans.

Moss, Stirling. A TURN AT THE WHEEL. New York: G.P. Putnam's Sons, 1961. 239 p.

This is a description of four years, 1957 to 1960, in which British racing cars and drivers achieved triumph after triumph. Moss has intermingled the story of these events with his own racing career during this period including some glimpses behind the scenes into his personal life.

Moss, Stirling, with Purdy, Ken. ALL BUT MY LIFE. New York: E.P. Dutton and Co., 1963. 239 p. Appendix. B/w photos.

An excellent biography, this book is filled with tale after tale not only of Moss the driver but Moss the man. His life both on and off the track are covered so that the reader sees a picture of a total man not just the part of him that takes the checkered flag. The appendix lists every race Moss ran from 1948 to 1961 and how he finished.

Mutch, Ronnie. NIKI LAUDA AND THE GRAND PRIX GLADIATORS. London: Sphere Books, 1977. 128 p. Paperbound.

This is a superficial look at Grand Prix racing with the author paying less attention to Niki Lauda than the title would indicate. He covers Lauda's near-fatal accident and dwells on racing as a "blood sport." There are interviews with James Hunt and Jody Scheckter. The author seems to be a "Johnny come lately" to the sport and is not familiar enough with drivers' names to realize that he has misspelled many.

Nolan, William F. PHIL HILL: YANKEE CHAMPION-FIRST AMERICAN TO WIN THE DRIVING CHAMPIONSHIP OF THE WORLD. New York: G.P. Putnam's Sons, 1962. 256 p.

Nolan presents the biography of the first American to win the driving championship of the world. This swiftly paced book follows Hill from his inital experience behind the wheel of a car to the tragic accident at Monza in 1961 that won him his crown. It covers his first crash in Mexico, his duels with Stirling Moss and the Marquis de Portago, his attempts to earn a ride with the Ferrari team, and his 1961 racing battles with Count Von Trips. A table at the end of the book outlines Hill's international successes from 1954 to 1962.

Pritchard, Anthony. THE WORLD CHAMPIONS: GIUSEPPE FARINA TO JACKIE STEWART. New York: Macmillan Co., 1972. 253 p. Appendix. B/w photos.

This is a series of biographies of the thirteen men who won the world driver's championship from 1950 to 1973. Tossed in is a chapter on Stirling Moss who was runner-up five times before he retired from racing due to injury. There is little new about these men to be found here but the known facts have been competently presented. Besides Moss, Farina, Fangio, Ascari, Hawthorn, Brabham, both Hills (Graham and Phil), Clark, Surtees, Hulme, Stewart, Rindt, and Fittipaldi are profiled. An appendix lists the top six drivers in points from 1950 to 1973.

Pruller, Heinz. JOCHEN RINDT, THE STORY OF A WORLD CHAMPION. Translated from the German by Peter Easton. London: William Kimber, 1970. 207 p.

Pruller was a friend of Rindt's and a racing journalist, and so presents an interesting and revealing portrait of a complex individual and an equally complex sport. All the joys, frustrations, and tragedies that are a part of any form of motorsport are recreated. Pruller also discloses that Rindt had planned to continue with Lotus and defend his championship before the tragic accident which ended his promising career. This is an excellent illustrated biography that will probably become a classic.

Revson, Peter, and Mandel, Leon. SPEED WITH STYLE: THE AUTOBIOGRAPHY OF PETER REVSON. Garden City, N.Y.: Doubleday and Co., 1974. 221 p. Appendix. Col. and b/w photos.

Revson and Mandel combine to relate the story of Peter's career in racing. Emphasis is on Formula I, but sports car and Indianapolis type racing are also covered. Fast paced and well written, the book gives an insight into the sport and Revson the man--a rare feat in racing biographies.

Scheckter, Jody. JODY: AN AUTOBIOGRAPHY. Johannesburg, South Africa: Hugh Keartland Publishers, 1976. 128 p.

Touted as an autobiography of Jody Scheckter, this book in reality leans toward being an overall view of Grand Prix racing by a man who lives in the midst of it. True, Jody does talk a bit about his youth and traces his racing growth, but never is Jody the man revealed. The book lacks spirit. Its worth lies in the chapters devoted to the sport itself--chapters on the designers, the mechanics, and the sponsors. A three-page appendix shows diagrams of some of the racing circuits of the world. However, the diagram of the Indianapolis Motor Speedway is inaccurate.

Stewart, Jackie, and Dymock, Eric. JACKIE STEWART: WORLD CHAMPION. New York: Henry Regnery, 1970. 191 p. Photos.

Jackie teams with Eric Dymock to tell the story of his climb from an amateur Scottish team driver to his ride with Ken Tyrrell and the top of the mountain--the world driving title. With much firsthand commentary by Jackie, the book captures the color and flavor of contemporary Grand Prix competition.

Stewart, Jackie, and Manso, Peter. FASTER! A RACER'S DIARY. New York: Farrar, Straus and Giroux, 1972. 239 p.

This is a book based on a diary kept by Jackie Stewart during 1970, oddly enough the year he didn't win the World Driver's Championship (he won in 1969 and 1971). This book shows the way a driver feels before a race, the frustrations that come when he doesn't win, his relationship with his mechanics, and his relationships with other drivers. The diary touches on Stewart's feelings when Jochen Rindt and Piers Courage are killed. This is an interesting study of a Grand Prix driver.

Tanner, Hans. GREAT RACING DRIVERS OF THE WORLD. New York: Sports Car Press, 1958. 126 p. Illus.

This book contains brief career sketches of the leading Grand Prix drivers of racing's past. From Ascari to Viloresi, thirty-seven drivers are covered. Most of the sketches are about three pages long.

D. OTHER FORMULA RACING

Brittan, Nick. THE FORMULA FORD BOOK: HOW IT STARTED, HOW IT GREW AND HOW YOU TACKLE IT TODAY. Newfoundland, N.J.: Haessner, 1978. 144 p. Photos.

Brittan gives an overview of the Formula Ford class and explains how to get started, what a season will cost, how to set up and prepare a car, driving techniques, and how to find a sponsor. There is also an interesting section on how to drive some well-known British tracks. Grand Prix stars James Hunt, Tom Pryce, Emerson Fittipaldi, and Jody Scheckter have also contributed to the book.

Morrow, Harry. FORMULA JUNIOR GUIDE. New York: Sports Car Press, 1961. 128 p.

This is an interesting discussion of a Formula which no longer exists. Morrow describes the cars, engines, chassis, and suspension setups. Much of the information applies only to Formula Junior but some techniques could be transferred to Formula II. The book is valuable from a historical and informational viewpoint.

Olney, Ross R., and Grable, Ron. THE RACING BUGS; FORMULA VEE AND SUPER VEE. New York: G.P. Putnam's Sons, 1974. 127 p.

Olney and Grable offer a simplified presentation of the history, growth, color, and regulations surrounding Formula Vee and Super Vee racing.

Smith, Brian. HOW TO START SINGLE SEATER RACING: GO FORMULA FORD. Cambridge, Mass.: Robert Bentley, 1970. 134 p.

Formula Ford is a class growing in popularity and is an excellent proving ground for young drivers. Smith provides a good illustrated look at the class and tells how to get started in it.

Williamson, H.W. HOT AND COOL VW'S: BUGGIES, FORMULA VEE'S AND SPECIALS. Modern Sports Car Series. New York: Sports Car Press, 1970. 125 p. Indexes.

This is an excellent monograph on a hard-to-find racing topic--the use of VW parts in the racing of dune buggies, Formula Vees, and other special racing machines. There is attention paid to mechanical procedures along with clear diagrams, and pictures. Indexes include a listing of Buggy and Vee Manufacturers and a listing of Formula Vee Associations.

E. SPORTS CAR RACING

Abodaher, David J. MAG WHEELS AND RACING STRIPES. New York: Julian Messner, 1973. 159 p. Glossary. B/w photos.

This work relates the description and background development of the cars used in American sports car racing rather than a description of racing itself. The book is aimed at a young adult audience but is well done and could appeal to an adult who is getting his feet wet in the world of sports car racing. There is good coverage of the sports cars of the 60s--the Mustang, the Camaro, the Plymouth Road Runner, and so forth.

AUTOCAR, ed. FIFTY YEARS OF LE MANS RACING. London: AUTOCAR, 1973. 76 p. Photos.

The editors have compiled an interesting photo album with accompanying text, covering events from 1923 to 1972. The material has been culled from the British weekly AUTOCAR. This is a fascinating compilation of old articles and photos, effectively tracing the evolution of this classic event.

Batchelor, Dean. FERRARI: THE EARLY BERLINETTAS AND COMPETITION COUPES. Newfoundland, N.J.: Haessner, 1974. 96 p. Drwgs., photos.

This volume, the first in a series on Ferrari models covers the 166/195/212 MM body, 340 Mexico body, 375 Mille Miglia body, the 250 GT, and several other 250 GT body styles. Photographs and scale drawings add to the value of the work. Specifications are also included. The competition history of each car is also discussed.

______. FERRARI: THE EARLY SPYDERS AND COMPETITION ROADSTERS. Newfoundland, N.J.: Haessner, 1975. 128 p. Drwgs., photos.

This is the second of a series on Ferrari competition and production models and includes the 166MM and SC, 250 Mille Miglia, 750 Monza and 860 Monza, the 118 and 121 Le Mans, 500 Testa Rossa, and the 196 Dino among others. Photographs and scale drawings make it a valuable work. Competition histories are included.

______. FERRARI: THE GRAN TURISMO AND COMPETITION BERLINETTAS. Newfoundland, N.J.: Haessner, 1977. 96 p. Drwgs., photos.

This is the third of a series dealing with specific Ferrari models. In this one, Batchelor has included the 250 GTO Series I and II, the 250 LM, 330 P2/3/4, 312 P, 275 GTB/C, and the 365GTB/4 "Daytona" among others. Photographs and scale drawings are again the predominate feature of the work.

Beeching, Jeanne. THE LAST SEASON: THE LIFE OF BRUCE McLAREN. Newfoundland, N.J.: Haessner, 1972. 232 p. Illus.

A biography of the famous racing driver and car builder who was killed 2 June 1970 in England, the book follows him through the five months of his last racing season. The reader sees him as he races, makes public appearances, and functions as a husband and father. There is a touch of humor blended with the business of racing.

Bochroch, Albert. AMERICANS AT LE MANS; AN ILLUSTRATED HISTORY OF THE 24 HOUR RACE FROM 1923 TO 1975 WITH EMPHASIS ON AMERICAN DRIVERS AND CARS. Tucson, Ariz.: Aztex Corp., 1976. 224 p. Index. Bibliography. B/w photos.

Bochroch presents a history of Le Mans with heavy emphasis on U.S. cars and drivers, particularly the efforts of Briggs Cunningham and Ford Motor Company. One appendix lists all American cars, their drivers, year competed, and finishing positions with a second giving the same information by driver.

Brittan, Nick. HOW TO GO SALOON CAR RACING. Newfoundland, N.J.: Haessner, 1968. 128 p.

British emphasis, but this is an interesting book on how to get started in production cars. Brittan is a knowledgeable racing writer.

Crump, Richard, and de la Rive Box, Rob. MASERATI: SPORTS, RACING & GT CARS 1926-1975. Foreword by Stirling Moss. Yeovil, Engl.: G.T. Foulis, 1975. 300 p. Illus., photos.

This is an illustrated history of the Maserati. It includes recorded models as well as some previously unknown models. The description of each model provides technical specifications and much detail of interest to Maserati buffs. There is a chronological arrangement.

Donohue, Mark, with Valkenburgh, Paul Van. THE UNFAIR ADVANTAGE. New York: Dodd, Mead and Co., 1975. 305 p. Index. Photos.

This is an autobiography of Donohue with emphasis on his career and the cars he drove, designed, and worked with. Much of the book deals with his long and successful relationship with Roger Penske.

Filby, Peter. TVR: SUCCESS AGAINST THE ODDS. London: Wilton House Gentry, 1976. 224 p. Index. Photos.

TVR, which has only a bit over a twenty-year history, has already established itself as an outstanding handmade specialist sports car. This book is an in-depth history of these unique cars including their racing history complete with Tommy Entwistle's Freddie Dixon Trophy wins. Specifications are an added boon.

Finn, Joel E. MASERATI: THE POSTWAR SPORTS RACING CARS. Minneapolis: Motorbooks International, 1977. 220 p. Photos.

Finn includes all the postwar models such as A6GCS, 150S, 250S, 350S, 450S, Tipo 60/61 63/64 Birdcages, and others. The Addenda provides production data, chassis and serial number locations, and body building and specification details. Finn gives a treasure trove of detail for Maserati lovers.

Fitch, John, with Nolan, William. ADVENTURE ON WHEELS: THE AUTOBIOGRAPHY OF A ROAD RACING CHAMPION. New York: G.P. Putnam's Sons, 1959. 284 p.

This is the story of sports car racer and team manager John Fitch. The book opens with his adventures as a fighter pilot in World War II, then drifts back to his boyhood and then ahead to his beginnings as a driver at Bridgehampton. From then on the reader is taken on a tour of both American and European arenas of competition. Interesting glimpses of the Nurburgring, Le Mans, Rheims, the Mille Miglia, and Monza are given.

Hinsdale, Peter. THE FABULOUS PORSCHE 917. Rev. 2d ed. Newfoundland, N.J.: Haessner, 1976. 112 p. Charts. Tables. Illus.

The 917 was one of the most successful cars Porsche ever built. It competed in every kind of event from Le Mans to club races and won many of them. The 917 dominated the Can-Am series and with its passing the 917 also faded from the scene. Hinsdale gives the complete history of the 917.

Hodges, David. THE FORD GT40 PROTOTYPES AND SPORTS CARS. London: Lionel Leventhal, 1970. 83 p. Drwgs., b/w photos.

A brief analytical look at the design, development, and competitions of the Ford GT40, this book possesses drawings and photos that add value to this work. Detailed specifications and the GT40 race record are included. It will probably be of interest only to those doing concentrated research on the GT40. Normal race fans would find this work dull.

Houston Bowden, Gregory A. MORGAN: FIRST AND LAST OF THE REAL SPORTS CARS. Foreword by Peter Morgan. New York: Dodd, Mead & Co., 1972. 191 p. Illus.

This is probably the most complete and accurate account of the Morgan automobile and the racing successes and failures yet done. Peter Morgan has allowed the author use of the company archives. This illustrated volume covers everything from how the cars are made to a competition history.

Johnes, Chris. ROAD RACE. New York: David McKay, 1977. 240 p. Index. Appendix. B/w photos.

ROAD RACE deals with only one form of motorsport-road racing in its most literal sense, races run on public roads, often for long distances. Course preparation, crowd control, insurance--all were minimal and helped to bring about the demise of even the biggest and oldest events. Too many spectators were killed or injured. The Mille Miglia and the Targa Florio make up most of the book but the Carrera Panamericana de Mexico and some Argentine events are included. The book also contains an appendix listing the most successful road racing cars from 1906 to 1973.

Ludvigsen, Karl E. THE INSIDE STORY OF THE FASTEST FORDS: THE DESIGN AND DEVELOPMENT OF FORD GT RACING CARS. Minneapolis: Motorbooks International, 1970. Photos.

Ludvigsen traces the history of the GT Ford from the G740 to G7-A. The book includes information on the Mark I, Mirage, Mark II, X-I, Mark 11A and 11B, Mark III, the J-Car, and the Mark IV. Construction details, aerodynamic tests, and race results are all given.

_____. THE WORLD'S MOST POWERFUL ROAD RACING CARS. Rev. ed. New York: Arco Publishing Co., 1973. 143 p.

This is the story of the Canadian American Challenge Cup series from its beginning in 1966 through 1972. The drivers, the tracks, and the cars are discussed and many of the races are analyzed in this book.

Moity, Christian. THE LE MANS 24 HOUR RACE, 1949-1973. Radnor, Pa.:

Chilton Book Co., 1974. 211 p. Index.

The second volume of the history of Le Mans, this big, lavishly illustrated book contains results, brief descriptions, and many excellent photos of every Le Mans race from 1949 to 1973. The results list the finishing position of each car, the reason it went out, the general classification by distance, and the Index of Thermal Efficiency winners.

Mull, Evelyn. WOMEN IN SPORTS CAR COMPETITION. New York: Sports Car Press, 1958. 105 p.

A woman driver explains where, how, and why women race. This book is limited to sports car racing but includes material on rallies, hillclimbs, and Speed Week at Nassau.

Orr, Frank. GEORGE EATON, FIVE MINUTES TO GREEN. Don Mills, Ont.: Longmans Canada, 1970. 149 p. Illus.

This is the story of George Eaton, a young Canadian race driver and his first season as a professional driver in competitive cars.

Pihera, Larry. THE MAKING OF A WINNER: THE PORSCHE 917. Philadelphia: J.B. Lippincott, 1972. 183 p.

Pihera covers the development of the Porsche 917 from a gleam in Ferry Porsche's eyes through the days it was unbeatable to its demise at the hands of the rules makers. Designed primarily for the Twenty-Four Hours of Le Mans, the 917 had a personality all its own. Early problems nearly doomed the car to obscurity, so the efforts of many men to turn it into a winner make fascinating reading.

Posey, Sam. THE MUDGE POND EXPRESS. New York: G.P. Putnam's Sons, 1976. 318 p.

Race driver Sam Posey writes of his life, his career, and the sport of speed as he sees it. His style makes interesting reading and the book is an articulate autobiography of one man and one point of view. Posey covers primarily Formula 5000, the Can Am, Trans-Am, and some Indy races.

Pourret, Jess G. THE FERRARI LEGEND: THE 250 GT COMPETITION BERLINETTA. Scarsdale, N.Y.: J.W. Barnes Jr. Publishing, 1977.

This is a translation of LE LEGENDE FERRARI.

Pritchard, Anthony. THE FERRARI V-12 SPORTS CARS, 1946-56. London: Lionel Leventhal, 1970. 80 p. Tables. Photos.

Pritchard is an authority on the Ferrari automobile and his treatment of the V-12 sports cars is excellent. He traces the technical development of the V-12s, gives a comprehensive racing history, and provides technical specifications and tables of results.

______. FORD VERSUS FERRARI: THE BATTLE FOR LE MANS. London: Pelham Books, 1968. 176 p. Illus.

Pritchard relates the epic struggle between the Dearborn giant and the legendary Modena marque for wins in the most famous and prestigious endurance race of them all.

______. THE RACING SPORTS CAR. New York: W.W. Norton, 1970. 368 p. Index.

Pritchard provides excellent coverage of the racing sports car from 1935 on. He covers such cars as the French Gordini, the Alfa Romeo, Disco Volante, the Matra, the Chaparral, the Lotus, the Cooper, the Scarab, the Shelby, and the Porsche. The book contains many specifications. Not a book for the average racing fan, this is a well-done serious work.

______. SPORTS CAR CHAMPIONSHIP. New York: W.W. Norton, 1972. 240 p. Appendixes. Illus.

This book covers the four-year period from 1968 to 1971. Some of the cars discussed are Porsche, Matra, Lola, and Ferrari. It was an interesting era with exciting cars, close competition, and new regulations. Pritchard traces the evolution of the cars and provides a close look at the competition. Appendixes cover race results and technical data.

Shelby, Carroll, as told to Bentley, John. THE COBRA STORY. New York: Trident Press, 1965. 272 p. Index. Illus.

The story of Carroll Shelby and the development of the Cobra automobile and its successes and failures on the major international circuits. Contains specifications of the 289 Cobra and the 427 Cobra and results of the FIA International Manufacturers Championship for Grand Touring cars in 1964 and 1965.

Stone, William S. A GUIDE TO AMERICAN SPORTS CAR RACING. Rev., 4th ed. Garden City, N.Y.: Doubleday and Co., 1971. 215 p. Glossary. Diags. Bibliography.

This is an excellent guide to the cars, driving techniques, and tracks of sports car racing. Section 1 contains a brief history of the sport, some tips on driving techniques and explanations of the less common types of sports car competition such as hill-climbs and gymkhanas. Section 2 deals with specific makes of sports cars giving specifications. Section 3 is a portfolio of racing photos, and section 4 is a description of sports car courses including a very helpful section on spectator areas, restrictions, travel directions, and where to write for information. A diagram of each course is included.

_____. GUIDE TO RACING DRIVERS SCHOOLS; HOW TO GET YOUR COMPETITION DRIVERS LICENSE. Modern Sports Car Series. New York: Sports Car Press, 1972. 121 p. Photos.

This is a guide to the proper method of becoming a SCCA race driver. The best portion of this book isn't its repetition of SCCA personal and car requirements, or its explanation of SCCA run driver's schools, but rather it is the two chapters devoted to the pro driving schools such as the Bob Bondurant School of High Performance, the Jim Russell Racing Driver's School, and the Bill Scott Racing School (among others).

Thornley, John. MAINTAINING THE BREED: THE SAGA OF MG RACING CARS. 3d ed. Cambridge, Mass.: Robert Bentley, 1971. 187 p.

Thornley traces the development of the MG from its beginnings up to the introduction of the MGA. He recounts the successes and failures of the various models and the development that went into each. He emphasizes the unsung heroes, the mechanics without whom no race car would turn a wheel. It is a book that will be enjoyed primarily by MG buffs.

Ulmann, Alec. THE SEBRING STORY. Chilton's Sebring Series. Philadelphia: Chilton Book Co., 1969. 203 p.

Ulmann covers all the twelve-hour endurance races held at Sebring--the teams, the results, the cars--up through 1969. The book contains some interesting photographs. Ulmann has been a Sebring official since its beginning in 1950.

Wilkinson, Sylvia. THE STAINLESS STEEL CARROT: AN AUTO RACING ODYSSEY. Boston: Houghton Mifflin, 1973. 335 p.

This is the story of eighteen months in the life of professional sports car driver, Californian John Morton. The author traveled with Morton's team, Brock Racing Enterprises, back and forth across the country during part of the 1971 and all of the 1972 season. It is an interesting look at the color of sports car racing and the stresses facing a man who is attempting to reach the top echelons of racing. There are many anecdotes about top racing drivers.

Yates, Brock. SUNDAY DRIVER. New York: Farrar, Straus and Giroux, 1972. 258 p.

This is an authentic portrayal of racing on the sports car circuit. It includes information on the Cannonball Baker Sea-to-Shining-Sea Memorial Trophy-Dash. Anyone who has ever towed a race car will love this.

Young, Eoin S. McLAREN! THE MAN, THE CARS AND THE TEAM. Newport Beach, Calif.: Bond, Parkhurst Publications, 1971. 272 p.

This book tells the story of Bruce McLaren, the development of the McLaren cars and the forging of a team strong enough to continue even though the man himself is gone. The work is rich in technical detail.

F. STOCK CAR RACING

Benyo, Richard. SUPERSPEEDWAY: THE STORY OF NASCAR GRAND NATIONAL RACING. New York: Mason/Charter, 1977. 280 p. Photos.

Benyo, the editor of STOCK CAR RACING magazine has keyed his discussion of Grand National racing to the 1976 season. Bill France and NASCAR are covered along with the major stars like Junior Johnson, Richard Petty, David Pearson, Cale Yarborough, the Woods Brothers, and others. One particular super speedway is discussed in detail--Talladega, an extremely fast track in Alabama.

______, ed. THE BOOK OF RICHARD PETTY. Alexandria, Va.: Lopez Automotive Group, 1976. 130 p. Paperbound. Photos.

A number of profiles on Richard Petty were taken from the pages of STOCK CAR RACING magazine and a few were commissioned especially for this collection. Many of the pieces cover specific races such as the 1975 World 600 and the 1976 Daytona 500. Of special interest are pieces on Maurice Petty, Richard's brother, and Dale Inman, his cousin. There is much Petty material available these days and this is better than most.

______. THE GRAND NATIONAL STARS. Alexandria, Va.: Lopez Automotive Group, 1975. 130 p. Paperbound. Photos.

A collection of biographies of NASCAR stars taken from the pages of STOCK CAR RACING. The quality is uneven as often happens when a variety of writers are represented but none of the material is dull. The major stars are represented but there are a few driver profiles not easily found elsewhere. These include Curtis Turner, Lennie Pond, Benny Parsons, and the best piece of the book--the piece on Fireball Roberts.

Berggren, Dick, ed. STOCK CAR RACING PHOTO SPECTACULAR: A

COMPENDIUM OF THE GREATEST STOCK CAR RACING PHOTOGRAPHY EVER PUBLISHED. Alexandria, Va.: Lopez Automotive Publications, 1977. 74 p. Paperbound. Col. and b/w photos.

Put out by the editors of STOCK CAR RACING magazine, this book contains many photos of competition crashes, but only from accidents in which injuries were slight or nonexistent. There is a small amount of text. It contains an interesting article on photographing stock car races.

Bledsoe, Jerry. THE WORLD'S NUMBER ONE, FLAT-OUT, ALL-TIME GREAT, STOCK CAR RACING BOOK. Garden City, N.Y.: Doubleday and Co., 1975. 335 p.

This is an excellent portrayal of the flavor and excitement of southern stock car racing. Bledsoe covers drivers (male and female), promoters, fans, big-time and small-time racing, even the death of Friday Hassler in prose that only a well-informed lover of the sport could manage. He goes beyond pure facts to the emotions living behind them.

Britt, Bloys, and France, Bill. THE RACING FLAG: NASCAR, THE STORY OF GRAND NATIONAL RACING. New York: Pocket Books, 1965. 84 p. Photos.

Written by a veteran race reporter, and the founder and guiding light of NASCAR, this brief book contains a short history of stock car racing, accounts of nine famous races and photos, and biographical sketches of some of NASCAR's star drivers. Also included are descriptions of the big NASCAR tracks and a listing of some of the smaller ones. The officials, scorers, car-building basics, and racing terms are mentioned briefly.

Butterworth, W.E. THE HIGH WIND: THE STORY OF NASCAR RACING. New York: Grosset and Dunlap, 1971. 95 p. Index. Appendix. B/w photos.

Usually an author of novels dealing with stock car racing, Butterworth has this time written a history of NASCAR, beginning with the first races in the United States through the 1970 NASCAR season. He had access to NASCAR files and the association's full cooperation. He also talked to many participants, attended races, visited the garages and pit areas, and in general did a thorough job. The 1971 NASCAR rule book is included as an appendix.

Engel, Lyle Kenyon, ed. THE COMPLETE BOOK OF NASCAR STOCK CAR RACING. Rev. ed. New York: Four Winds Press, 1974. 184 p. Glossary. B/w photos.

A general book that looks at the various NASCAR divisions, tracks, and drivers. It covers the Grand National Circuit, the Modified Circuit, the Sportsman Circuit, the Hobby Division, and the Pacific Coast Division of NASCAR. The book is not indexed.

_____. RACING TO WIN--WOOD BROTHERS STYLE. New York: Arco Publishing Co., 1974. 158 p. Illus.

An illustrated portrait with text by Jim Hunter of the famous Wood Brothers pit crew, this is an absorbing look at the part a crew can play in the fortunes of such racing greats as A.J. Foyt, Curtis Turner, Jim Clark, and David Pearson.

_____. STOCK CAR RACING U.S.A. Text by Jim Hunter. Edited by George Engel and Marla Ray. New York: Dodd, Mead and Co., 1973. 191 p.

This book covers most of the prominent drivers in stock car racing from the beginning to the current stars and the cars that carried them to glory.

Haener, Donald. HOMETOWN STOCK CAR RACING. Erie, Pa.: Discovery Enterprises, 1975. 89 p. Photos.

This interesting book deals with the exciting, highly competitive world of "outlaw" racing primarily on the small tracks of the eastern United States. It covers the sportsmen and late model stockers.

Higdon, Hal. SHOWDOWN AT DAYTONA. New York: G.P. Putnam's Sons, 1976. 159 p. Index. B/w photos.

This book is billed as the "inside story" of the 1975 Daytona 500 but it emerges as a rather dull race report brightened by a few quotes and interviews. There have been several stock car racing books that do a superior job of catching the color and flavor of the southern scene. This book falters in comparison.

Jackson, Robert B. STOCK CAR RACING: GRAND NATIONAL COMPETITION. New York: Harry Z. Walck, 1968. 64 p.

This is a brief account of stock car racing at its highest level, Grand National Competition. Jackson aims at the young adult market. The sport itself, Grand National cars, and the men who drive them are covered. The Southern 500 at Darlington International Raceway in 1966 is recounted. Short, but interesting particularly to teenagers bitten by the car bug, it's a good book for a reluctant reader.

Krishef, Robert K. THE DAYTONA 500. Minneapolis: Lerner Publications Co., 1976. 55 p. Illus.

This easy-to-read book recalls many of the events and drivers who made the Daytona 500 the famous event it is today. It includes material on Bill France, safety rules, and racing associations.

Libby, Bill. HEROES OF STOCK CAR RACING. New York: Random House, 1975. 152 p. Index. B/w photos.

These brief biographies of twelve stock car drivers including Lee and Richard Petty, Fireball Roberts, Freddie Lorenzen, Joe Weatherly, A.J. Foyt, and Curtis Turner have been written for a junior high school audience. The chapters contain no new information but are accurate.

Libby, Bill, with Petty, Richard. "KING RICHARD": THE RICHARD PETTY STORY. Garden City, N.Y.: Doubleday and Co., 1977. 322 p. B/w photos.

Richard Petty is the acknowledged king of NASCAR stock car racing. But no one gets to the top alone and Richard's story is also the story of his family, his friends, his competitors, and his sport. Libby provides much more insight into Petty the man than is usual with most racing biographies. It contains an abundance of quotes, interviews, and comments from everyone involved with the Pettys and stock car racing. The biography continues through 1976 and gives a preview of 1977.

Parsons, Benny, and Smith, Steve. STOCK CAR DRIVING TECHNIQUES. Rev. Santa Ana, Calif.: Steve Smith Autosports, 1977. 96 p. B/w photos.

Every aspect of competition driving is covered in this small book written by 1973 NASCAR Grand National champion Benny Parsons. His instructions include the basics of competition driving, special instructions on driving the dirt tracks, super-speedways, and the individual Grand National Circuits, plus a chapter devoted to driving techniques used when a race driver gets into trouble.

Petty, Richard. GRAND NATIONAL: THE AUTOBIOGRAPHY OF RICHARD PETTY. Chicago: Henry Regnery, 1971. 212 p. Illus.

This is the story of the Pettys and their Plymouths and NASCAR Grand National racing. Richard is the central figure, but the rest of the Petty team get their share of credit.

______. KING OF THE ROAD. New York: Macmillan Co., 1977. 200 p. Drwgs., col. and b/w photos.

The strong point of this book is the illustrations. The photos record Richard Petty, his crew, his family, his fans, and

NASCAR racing in detail. Griesdieck succeeds in capturing the excitement of racing and the camaraderie of its participants. Richard's comments and stories of his racing adventures make good reading and the easy-going attitude which makes Petty a southern folk hero comes through very well.

Silber, Mark. RACING STOCK. Garden City, N.Y.: Doubleday and Co., 1976. 161 p. B/w photos.

A polished piece of writing, this is well researched and well presented. Silber has touched all the bases of stock car racing--drivers, crews, beauty queens, fans, wives, announcers, and the press. He hasn't relied on library research for his material but gone straight to the sources. His work abounds in quotes. There is material here that is hard to find elsewhere--profiles on Darryl Waltrip, Bruce Jacobi, and Pat Singer. It also contains a rare chapter on powder puff driving.

STOCK CAR DRIVERS. Alexandria, Va.: Lopez Automotive Group, 1977. 82 p. Paperbound. Photos.

A collection of sketches of drivers, most of whom are stock car drivers. Some are still racing and others are retired. Some are or were successful and some not so successful. Among those included are Ron Slade, Joe Mihalic, Skip Manning, Ted Horn, and Ned Jarrett. This is an interesting collection.

G. DRAG RACING

Bortstein, Larry. HOT RODS AND DRAG RACING. Mahwah, N.J.: Troll Associates, 1974. 32 p. Photos. by Leslie Lovett.

A brief description of the drag racing scene and the kinds of cars involved.

Coombs, Charles. DRAG RACING. New York: William Morrow and Co., 1970. 96 p. Index. Photos.

A brief introduction to the sport aimed primarily at young adults, the book discusses car classification, pit activity, operation of the strip, and driver training. The last chapter describes the actual running of a race.

Edmonds, I.G. DRAG RACING FOR BEGINNERS. Indianapolis: Bobbs-Merrill Co., 1972. 146 p. Drwgs., photos.

Edmonds introduces the cars, drivers, classes, and rules of drag racing. The book is aimed at younger readers from grade nine upwards.

_____. HOT RODDING FOR BEGINNERS. New York: Barnes and Noble, 1970. 181 p. Illus.

Edmonds has written a basic book on the sport which covers engines, tools, equipment, swaps, customizing, and competition. This is a basic book for the young man or woman getting started.

Engel, Lyle Kenyon. COMPLETE BOOK OF FUEL AND GAS DRAGSTERS. New York: Four Winds Press, 1968. 168 p. Glossary.

The author covers some of the major developments in drag racing when speeds jumped to two-hundred-plus mph and six-second runs were achieved. "Funny cars," jet cars, and wheel standing specials, match races, altereds, coups, and modifieds are all part of the story.

_____. THE COMPLETE BOOK OF STOCK-BODIED DRAG RACING. New York: Four Winds Press, 1970. 104 p. Index. Glossary. B/w photos.

Three-quarters of the total annual drag strip entry are stock cars of various types. Produced by Engel and the editorial staff of AUTO RACING magazine, the book is a fairly comprehensive history of stock-bodied drag racing and the classes set up by the sanctioning bodies. Detailed information on stockers, super stockers, factory experimentals, modified production, gas coupes, and street roadsters is provided.

Garlits, Don, and Yates, Brock. KING OF THE DRAGSTERS: THE STORY OF BIG DADDY "DON" GARLITS. Philadelphia: Chilton Book Co., 1967. 217 p. Photos.

Don Garlits, with the expert help of racing writer Brock Yales, relates the development of his career from his high school years in Tampa to winning the "Mr. Eliminator USA" title in 1966. Though most of the book deals with his career, he talks about himself and his family as well. He also has some very definite things to say about staying in school and studying, emphasizing the need for a strong math and physics background for successful car building.

Higdon, Hal. SIX SECONDS TO GLORY: DON PRUDHOMME'S GREATEST DRAG RACE. New York: G.P. Putnam's Sons, 1975. 159 p. Index. Photos.

A detailed and exciting account of Don "The Snake" Prudhomme's attempt to win a fourth victory at the NHRA Nationals in 1973. Higdon captures the excitement and thrill of big-league drag racing.

Jackson, Robert B. QUARTER-MILE COMBAT: THE EXPLOSIVE WORLD OF DRAG RACING. New York: Henry Z. Walck, 1975. 71 p.

A brief introductory look at drag racing written in simple language and packed with much information in a short space. There is material on trophy runs, pro stockers, and top fuelers. Length allows only the surface to be skimmed, but this is nicely done.

Jordan, Pat. "Cha-Cha and Her Time Machine." In his BROKEN PATTERNS, pp. 143-54. New York: Dodd, Mead and Co., 1977.

In this book on famous female athletes who have broken out of the conventional mold, a chapter on Shirley "Cha Cha" Muldowney is a natural. The article covers Shirley from her high school days of skipping school through her start in racing with her then-husband and her professional success as a top-ranking drag racer. Many quotes make this excellent.

MacPherson, Tom. DRAGGING, DRIVING AND BASIC CUSTOMIZING. New York: G.P. Putman's Sons, 1972. 160 p. Index. B/w photos.

A hodge-podge of information for the young driver that bounces back and forth between street driving and drag racing. There is basic material presented on body customizing, the competition powerplants, and opportunities for competition for the beginning driver. The last chapter is a valuable glossary entitled "Dragging and Automotive Jargon."

Madigan, Tom. THE LONER: THE STORY OF A DRAG RACER. Foreword by James Garner. Englewood Cliffs, N.J.: Prentice-Hall, 1974. 117 p. B/w photos.

This is a story of drag racing incorporated into the life of drag champion Tony Nancy. Not only is Nancy's career as a racer detailed but also his colorful car upholstering for race and special cars. You will recognize many Hollywood names among his clientele.

Olney, Ross R. GREAT DRAGGING WAGONS. New York: G.P. Putnam's Sons, 1970. 160 p. Index. B/w photos.

This easily read book is a series of short chapters with pictures on some of the most famous drag racing cars ever known. Such cars as Little Red Wagon, Green Monster, Rambunctious, Wynn's Jammer, and Super Chief are detailed including colorful racing incidents, mechanical factors and famous drivers. The last portion of the book is a gallery of dragging wagons in words and pictures. Short two to three-page descriptions of additional drag cars are given. An excellent index makes this a valuable guide to information not easily found.

_____. KINGS OF THE DRAG STRIP. New York: G.P. Putnam's Sons, 1968. 192 p. Index. Glossary.

This book contains short biographical sketches of twelve of the nation's top drag racing drivers including Don Prudhomme, Tommy Ivo, Art Malone, Mickey Thompson, Gas Ronda, Tom McEwen, Don Garlits, and others. It also contains a list of drag racing classes.

Parks, Wally. DRAG RACING: YESTERDAY AND TODAY; THE STORY OF THE FASTEST SPORT IN THE WORLD. New York: Trident Press, 1966. 240 p. Index. Glossary. B/w photos.

Written by the man most responsible for the success of drag racing, this book covers the early years of the sport, the growth, the cars, experimental tires, and fuels and engines as well as the emphasis on safety. Particularly interesting was the selling job the early organizers had to do to citizens, law enforcement agencies, and the kids themselves.

Puleo, Nicole. DRAG RACING. Fearon Racing Series. Belmont, Calif.: Published for Lear Siegler by Fearon Publishers, 1974. 47 p. Col. photos.

This material is easily understood. It is a basic booklet that portrays the color and excitement of a typical day at the dragstrip. Descriptions of various types of dragsters are given.

Radlauer, Edward. DRAG RACING: QUARTER MILE THUNDER. New York: Abelard-Schuman, 1966. 152 p. Index. Glossary. Drwgs., photos.

This book begins with a brief history of drag racing and the developments of the 1960s. Considerable attention is given to safety. Safety requirements for the car, the driver, and the track are set by the sanctioning body. The various classes in drag racing are listed and explained, and an actual event is described.

Sox, Ronnie, and Martin, Buddy. THE SOX AND MARTIN BOOK OF DRAG RACING. Chicago: Henry Regnery, 1974. 227 p. Glossary. Col. and b/w photos.

Sox and Martin tell the story of their highly successful team, give tips on driving and race car engineering, and cover the history of the sport. Race records, explanations of car classes, and a discussion of sponsorships are included.

Stambler, Irwin. HERE COME THE FUNNY CARS. New York: G.P. Putnam's Sons, 1976. 127 p. Index. B/w photos.

This is another in a long line of basic books on drag racing. This volume reveals little not covered in previous works. There is a brief history of the sport followed by some basic drag racing explanations. The remainder of the book is devoted to short anecdotes about famous name drivers and their exploits. Good biographical data on "Cha Cha" Muldowney is included.

SUPER STOCK AND DRAG ILLUSTRATED PHOTO GREATS. Alexandria, Va.: Lopez Automotive Group, 1977. 74 p. Paperbound. Col. and b/w photos.

A collection of drag racing photos selected by the staff of SUPER STOCK AND DRAG ILLUSTRATED. The photos were taken by free-lance photographers and cover all aspects of drag racing. Funny cars and rails predominate. All the photos are spectacular.

WINTER DRAGS. Alexandria, Va.: Lopez Automotive Group, 1977. Paperbound. Col. and b/w photos.

Covers the drag events which inaugurate the drag racing season each year. Events included are Phoenix, Tucson, and Pomona. Excellent action photographs are accompanied by commentary.

H. KARTING

Burgess, Alan. GOING KARTING. 4th rev. ed. Chislehurst, Engl.: Lodgemark Press, 1973. 24 p.

A complete but brief survey of karting in Great Britain, this book has been prepared by an expert.

______, comp. INTERNATIONAL 100CC KART ENGINES--1975, 1976 AND 1977. Chislehurst, Engl.: Lodgemark Press, 1975. 44 p. Illus.

Burgess gives the complete specifications and drawings of more than ten kart engines.

Day, Dick. THE COMPLETE BOOK OF KARTING. Englewood Cliffs, N.J.: Prentice-Hall, 1961. 179 p. Index. Photos.

Gives a brief history of karting, tips on selecting a kart, how to build a kart on your own, how to drive one, and where to race. Written with help of the editors of KART magazine, the book also discusses maintenance, laws affecting karting, and several kinds of special karts. It also includes rules and regulations of the Go Kart Club of America, but these have undoubtedly changed.

McFarland, Kenton D., and Sparks, James C., Jr. MIDGET MOTORING AND KARTING. New York: E.P. Dutton and Co., 1961. 159 p. Illus.

This not a book on the actual world of go-kart racing but a well-done look at how to build a kart. It is not a manual for the uninitiated mechanically, but the material has good illustrations. There are separate chapters on engine selection, chassis, wheels and brakes, suspension, bodies, safety, and commercial karts. There is not great deal of literature available in this field and this book is worth consulting even if it is beginning to age.

Radlauer, Edward. KARTING CHALLENGE. Los Angeles: Elk Grove Press, 1969. 69 p. Glossary. Col. photos.

This is a very elementary entry on kart racing but little is available on this subject. Written in the first person from a boy's point of view, the book tells the story of buying and racing a kart.

Smith, Leroi "Tex." KARTING. New York: Arco Publishing Co., 1971. 215 p.

Smith explains what karting is and how it began, how to choose a kart and the differences between sprint, enduro, formula, concession, and fun karts. There are chapters on the mechanics behind karts including chassis, wheels, brakes, engines, exhaust systems, and fuel tanks. Material on how to drive karts, what protective clothes to wear, and a special final chapter explaining the mathematical background needed for karts makes this an excellent work.

I. OTHER RACING TYPES

Fox, Jack C. THE MIGHTY MIDGETS. Speedway, Ind.: Carl Hungness Publishing, 1977. 302 p. Photos.

Fox has done an excellent history of midget racing from 1933 to 1976. The midgets were born in California in 1933 and Fox tells of the steady growth in crowds, car owners, and promotors. He tells of the glory days immediately after World War II and then of a decline, controversy, and feuds. One can read about midget racing's brightest stars--Bill Belleridge, Shorty Templeman, Ronney Householder, Freddy Agabashian, and others. The tracks, too, like Ascot, Gilmore Stadium, and the Nutley Vilodrome are here, too. There is an obvious emphasis on West Coast racing and so coverage of other parts of the country is weak. No matter--this is still an excellent book. The photographs add a great deal to the book.

Johnson, Norman T., and Gummis, Gordon. THE OFF-ROAD RACER (1976).

Las Vegas: G. and J. Publishing Co., 1976. 271 p. Photos.

One of the most complete books yet published on off-road racing, this one covers the history and growth of the sport as well as the history of several of the major organizations and events like the Mint 400 and the Baja 1000. There is also an extensive section of driver profiles. The more prominent drivers have detailed information provided along with a photo. The remaining drivers have basic biographical data given along with a brief career summary and a photo. Map routes of some of the Baja races and the 1976 Mint 400 are given. It's very complete.

Norris, Monty. OFF ROAD RACING. Edited by George Engel and Marla Ray. New York: Dodd, Mead and Co., 1974. 148 p. Index. B/w photos.

Produced by Lyle Kenyon Engel, this book tells the story of off-road racing from its beginning in the early 60s down to the 1972 season. It gives ideas on how to get started, what to expect during an event, and a few tips on how to build an off-road vehicle. The Mexican 1000 events run, through Baja, California, are described.

Popp, Dennis. ICE RACING. Fearon Racing Series. Belmont, Calif.: Published for Lear Siegler by Fearon Publishers, 1974. 39 p. Illus.

This booklet examines an unusual form of auto racing. It features an article on its most famous event: the Carnival Cup 100 Mile Race, detailing the preparation and practice for the race, and the race itself. It also provides extended coverage of the International Ice Racing Association.

Radlauer, Edward, and Radlauer, R.S. BUGGY-GO-ROUND. New York: Franklin Watts, 1971. 47 p. Index. Glossary. Illus.

This book covers the sport of dune buggy racing on a closed dirt circuit. The material is presented in a simple straight forward style making it suitable for all ages and educational levels. It explains tracks, equipment, and racing organization setup.

Scalzo, Joe. STAND ON THE GAS: SPRINT CAR RACING IN AMERICA. Englewood Cliffs, N.J.: Prentice-Hall, 1974. 203 p. Illus.

Joe Scalzo has written the best book on sprint car racing yet published. Profusely illustrated, this text catches the color of the drivers, the tracks, and the machines in a manner that leaves the reader ready to grab the family car and head for the nearest sprint race. Nowhere else will you find the famous racing duels of Gary Bettenhausen and Larry Dickson so well chronicled. You will read all the famous sprint names past and present--A.J. Foyt, Jim Hurtubise, Parnelli Jones, Jud Larson, Don Branson, Bob

Sweikert, Pat O'Conner, Jan Opperman, Tommy Hinnershitz, and Rollie Beale. This is not a book written from library research, but a book written by a man who knows the sport and is willing to share his knowledge and his love.

Smith, Don. THE BAJA RUN: RACING FURY. Mahwah, N.J.: Troll Associates, 1976. 32 p. Col. and b/w photos.

Smith covers all the excitement and action of the annual Baja off-road race, the Mexican 1000. The book is aimed at a younger audience.

J. RACING TECHNOLOGY

BUILDING A RACE CAR PICTURE BY PICTURE. Santa Ana, Calif.: Steve Smith Autosports, 1976. 50 p. Photos.

This is primarily a collection of photographs of the construction details of many of the most successful stock cars built today. Pictures include shots of sportsmen, modifieds, and Grand National cars. The photos show structure, design, component placement, and various stages of construction. Photos are carefully captioned.

Campbell, Colin. DESIGN OF RACING SPORTS CARS. Cambridge, Mass.: Robert Bentley, 1973. 257 p. Diags.

A book intended for the technically minded race enthusiast, it covers tires, suspensions, frame and body, engines, transmissions, aerodynamics, braking, and handling. It contains many diagrams to illustrate the text, and concerns primarily sports cars and Grand Touring cars.

______. THE SPORTS CAR: ITS DESIGN AND PERFORMANCE. 3d rev. ed. Cambridge, Mass.: Robert Bentley, 1970. 305 p. Tables. Charts. Graphs. Diags. B/w photos.

A highly technical engineering book, this work discusses the modern sports car in all its aspects. Engines, chassis, suspension, transmissions, and brakes are given through coverage. New developments in aerodynamics, engines, and tires are discussed. A new method of calculating potential acceleration of a projected sports car is given, and new tables give acceleration and maximum speeds of representative modern sports cars.

______. THE SPORTS CAR ENGINE: ITS TUNING AND MODIFICATION. Cambridge, Mass.: Robert Bentley, 1964. 322 p.

Although the materials in this book could be used to tune cars for street use, most users would want to supertune competition engines. Some of the specifics are dated but the basic theory is still applicable. Not written with the weekend mechanic in mind, the author presupposes a considerable knowledge of engines. He covers all aspects of fine tuning, ignition, fuel mixtures, carburetion, camshafts, supercharging, turbocharging, combustion, and troubleshooting. It has a British slant.

Christy, John. HOW TO BUILD HOT RODS AND RACE THEM. 2d ed. Indianapolis: Bobbs-Merrill Co., 1966. 303 p. Index. Photos.

Although somewhat dated, the book presents the basics and important specifics of the art of hot rodding. It would no longer be useful for the advanced rodder but the beginner will find much of the basic knowledge needed in this book. This book is readable and concise.

Costin, Michael, and Phipps, David. RACING AND SPORTS CAR CHASSIS DESIGN. 2d ed. Cambridge, Mass.: Robert Bentley, 1965. 147 p. Glossary. Appendixes.

Limited to the chassis and suspension this is a specialized work. Several types of chassis are analyzed and the design of eighteen successful cars are discussed. Lotus, Lola, Mercedes, Jaguar, Ferrari, and Maserati are among those covered. Illustrated with photos and diagrams, the book also contains appendixes on chassis, stress calculations, materials, and suspension calculations.

Ezzell, Peter, and Quan, John. BUILDING YOUR VW BASED DUNEBUGGY. San Diego: Quazell Technical, 1969. 79 p. Illus.

This technical manual contains material that can be used in readying dune buggies for racing. Chapters cover chassis, engine, transaxle, suspension, mounting the body, electrical designs and accessories, and finishing.

Finch, Richard. HOW TO KEEP YOUR CORVAIR ALIVE. New ed. Tucson, Ariz.: H.P. Books, 1977. 96 p. Paperbound.

Finch begins with family car maintenance and proceeds to full-race modifications for SCCA's D-Production class. Corvair buffs will appreciate this book.

Fisher, Bill. HOW TO HOTROD CORVAIRS. Rev. ed. Tucson, Ariz.: H.P. Books, 1969. 106 p. Paperbound. Photos.

This book contains much useful information on GM's Corvair engines. Although Corvairs are no longer made, there are still many on the roads and the engines are much in demand. Anyone working on a Corvair engine will find something in this book to help. All publications of this type from H.P. Books are heavily illustrated with photographs. It does presuppose some mechanical knowledge and is not indexed.

_____. HOW TO HOTROD VOLKSWAGENS. Tucson, Ariz.: H.P. Books, 1970. 160 p. Paperbound. B/w photos.

Typical of the titles published by H.P. Books, this one offers much detailed and useful information for the growing number of VW enthusiasts who have discovered the high performance potential of the VW engine. Formula Vee engine builders should beware--much of what is suggested in this book is illegal under SCCA rules. The author does presuppose mechanical know-how. No index is provided.

Fisher, Bill, and Waar, Bob. HOW TO HOTROD BIG-BLOCK CHEVYS. Rev. Tucson, Ariz.: H.P. Books, 1972. 160 p. Paperbound. B/w photos.

This is a performance manual which enables the mechanically minded race driver or the race mechanic to engineer performance from his big-block Chevy engine. The book contains the usual material found in a book of this type--carburetion, ignition, pistons, clutch and flywheel, and lubrication.

_____. HOW TO HOTROD SMALL-BLOCK CHEVYS. Tucson, Ariz.: H.P. Books, 1976. 193 p. Paperbound. Photos.

This excellent entry in the H.P. Books performance series covers all small-block engines 265 through 400 cubic inches. The photos are helpful, the instructions are clear. The instructions are not for the Sunday afternoon mechanic, however. The lack of an index hurts this one as it has others in the series. Many aspects of high performance and reliable tips are included.

Goddard, George. FAST TRACK: 1/4 MIDGET ENGINE HAND-BOOK. Ontario, Calif.: Goddard Enterprises, n.d. 62 p. Paperbound. Tables. Charts. Illus.

A booklet designed to aid beginners in the sport of quarter midget racing to understand the quarter midget engine, it covers carburetion, spark plugs, ignition systems, rings, ports, valves, tuning, and engine tools. There is a section on teardown and reassembly. Tables include a #35 Gear Ratio Chart, a #40 Gear Ratio Chart and a Tap/Drill chart along with illustrations.

Henry, Alan. THE 4-WHEEL DRIVES: RACING'S FORMULA FOR FAILURE? New York: Arco Publishing Co., 1975. 80 p. Photos.

Henry discusses the disastrous course of the rise of four-wheel drive on racing cars as tried by master car builders such as Lotus,

Matra, Cosworth, and McLaren. The book traces the trial-and-error methods, and shows how each designer tried and failed to successfully utilize the theoretical advantage of the four-wheel drive.

HIGH PERFORMANCE WITH FUEL INJECTORS. Santa Ana, Calif.: Steve Smith Autosports, 1971. 38 p. Illus.

This work is oriented toward Hilborn fuel injection systems, yet will provide the reader with a good basic introduction to fuel injection. It covers fuel pumps, metering valves, nozzles, filters, fuel lines, ram tubes, installation procedures, and maintenance and trouble shooting routines.

HOT ROD, ed. ENGINES. Los Angeles: Peterson Publishing Co., 1977. 96 p. Paperbound. Illus.

A magazine format presentation of tips to use on hot rod engines, the section headings include "Budget Performance Buildups," "Super Street Engines," "Turbocharging Secrets," "Ignition Tuning Tips," "For Racers Only," "The Fuel Systems," "Headwork," and the "Valve Train."

Humphreys, B.J., and Malewick, Douglas. ROCKET POWERED RACING VEHICLES USING HYDROGEN PEROXIDE OF 90% STRENGTH. Minneapolis: Motorbooks International, 1974. 99 p. Illus.

The book covers technical aspects of rocket power as applied to drag cars, land speed record cars, and other cars. It includes descriptions for and specifications of many rocket cars including Gary Gabelich's "Blue Flame." NHRA rules for rocket-propelled vehicles are given. Data on use of hydrogen peroxide as a fuel is provided.

Jenkins, Bill, with Schrieb, Larry. THE CHEVROLET RACING ENGINE. Santa Fe Springs, Calif.: S-A Design Company Publishing, 1976. 159 p. Diags. Photos.

Bill "Grumpy" Jenkins, a former drag racer turned mechanic and shop owner, provides most useful information for those racing Chevy engines. He discusses cylinder blocks, crankshafts, bearings, connecting rods, heads, valves, camshafts, induction, exhaust, ignition, and lubrication. The book is useful for Chevy buffs.

MacInnes, Hugh. TURBOCHARGERS. Tucson, Ariz.: H.P. Books, 1976. 192 p. Illus.

MacInnes covers turbo-design, sizing and matching, installation, controls, and street and race cars. Appendixes include kit makers and installers, a compression selection chart, and a horsepower increase chart.

Moss, Stirling, and Pomeroy, Laurence. DESIGN AND BEHAVIOR OF THE RACING CAR. London: William Kimber, 1963. 285 p. Photos. by Louis Klemantaki.

Although dated now, the book will remain somewhat of a classic because anything Stirling Moss has to say about race cars retains value. Racing cars have changed considerably in both design and behavior, but his is still excellent for the cars under discussion.

Murray, Spencer. PETERSEN'S BASIC ENGINE HOT RODDING. Los Angeles: Petersen Publishing Co., 1975. 192 p. Diags. Photos.

A basic book on engine hot rodding techniques, it gives hop-up tricks, blueprinting shortcuts, economy camshafts, turbos and injectors, modification techniques for crankshafts and rods, tool and gauge usage, and exhaust systems. Tuning hints are also given. This is a very basic book for the beginning hot rodder.

Pappas, John. OVAL TRACK CHASSIS DESIGN: THEORY AND PRACTICE. Vancouver, Wash.: Superior Books, 1977. 144 p. Diags. Charts.

A gold mine of practical information and theory on race car chassis design, the emphasis is on oval track racing. It's a good book for the do-it-yourself racer with a limited budget who wants to do a little more than use the stock setup. Frames, cages, suspension, roll bars, shocks, and brakes are among the topics covered.

Pershing, Bernard, ed. AERODYNAMICS OF SPORTS AND COMPETITION AUTOMOBILES: SECOND SYMPOSIUM. Minneapolis: Motorbooks International, 1975. 300 p. Drwgs., photos.

This work consists of the proceedings of the 1974 symposium of the American Institute of Aeronautics and Astronautics. Each article is done by an expert and covers such topics as the design of the Parnelli F1 wing, ground effects on a Can-Am car, aerodynamics on the Bonneville Salt Flats, and trapped vortex flow.

Petersen, Robert E. THE COMPLETE BOOK OF HOT RODDING. Englewood Cliffs, N.J.: Prentice-Hall, 1959. 224 p. Index. Glossary.

This is one of the earliest and best books on hot rodding and how to do it, good for the beginner. Horsepower, valve work, carburetion, compression ratios, supercharging, engine swapping, transmission work, and trouble-shooting techniques are basic to the art, and these chapters contain much that is still useful.

The section on racing tires should be disregarded.

Puhn, Fred. HOW TO MAKE YOUR CAR HANDLE. Tucson, Ariz.: H.P. Books, 1976. 197 p. Paperbound. Photos.

Puhn tells how to check the chassis settings, suspension and alignment, gives the set-up for drag racing, track and road courses, and provides much practical data, formulas, and instruction. The book is very informative.

Roe, Doug, and Fisher, Bill. ROCHESTER CARBURETORS. Tucson, Ariz.: H.P. Books, 1973. 296 p. Paperbound. Photos.

The authors cover the quadrajet, two barrel, and monojet. They explain how carburetors operate, the basic principles of carburetion, air and fuel requirements, performance and race tuning, and rebuilding.

Smith, Carroll. PREPARE TO WIN. Fallbrook, Calif.: Aero Publications, 1975. 175 p. Illus.

A road racer of much experience, Smith provides much information on car preparation. Topics covered include fasteners, plumbing, rivets and welding, metal work, braking, suspension, wheels, engines, gearboxes, alignment, and electrical work. An especially useful chapter covers records, paperwork, and organization. This book is a must for any successful race operation.

Smith, Le Roi. MAKE YOUR OWN HOT ROD. New York: Dodd, Mead and Co., 1971. 303 p.

This is exactly what the title implies. The chapters cover engines, clutches, transmissions, rear ends, chassis, suspensions, brakes, wheels, and tires. It describes fiberglass hotrods, custom painting, and racing. The book is an excellent source for the beginning race car builder.

Smith, Philip H. THE DESIGN AND TUNING OF COMPETITION ENGINES. 6th ed. Revised by David N. Wenner. Cambridge, Mass.: Robert Bentley, 1977. 517 p. Index.

A technical book on high performance engines, the first part deals with basic principles, mechanical construction, crankshaft design, carburetion, fuel injection, combustion, and problems of high speed operation. The rest of the chapters (5 through 21) discuss specific engines like the American V-8, Cosworth 426, the Volkswagen, and others. Other aspects are covered in detail like the cylinder heads, valve gears, supercharging, compression ratios, and piston and rings. The book also contains definitions, formulas, and abbreviations. It is not for a beginner.

Smith, Steve. ADVANCED RACE CAR SUSPENSION DEVELOPMENT. Santa Ana, Calif.: Steve Smith Autosports, 1974. 176 p. Appendixes. Illus.

This book is an excellent technical manual of interest to the professional racing mechanic. Among topics covered are rack and pinion steering, lateral control linkages, shock absorbers, weight distributions, and spring rates. Three appendixes contain math fundamentals, trig tables, and a glossary of terms. It is not for the beginner.

_____. ADVANCED RACE CAR SUSPENSION DEVELOPMENT WORKBOOK. Santa Ana, Calif.: Steve Smith Autosports. Paperbound.

The workbook was created specifically to accompany Smith's ADVANCED RACE CAR SUSPENSION DEVELOPMENT. All of the formulas covered in the book are presented and covered specifically, point by point. Pages have blanks for the user to fill in specific information for his car. Updated material has been added. Examples of a complete chassis analysis are also given.

_____. THE COMPLETE STOCK CAR CHASSIS GUIDE. Santa Ana, Calif.: Steve Smith Autosports, 1972. 32 p. Diags. Photos.

This advanced book on handling and suspension for stock cars provides useful information for the experienced mechanic. It covers such points as superspeedway aerodynamics, shock absorbers, racing tires, roll cages, and sorting and testing a chassis. It is clear and concise.

_____. RACE CAR FABRICATION AND PREPARATION. Santa Ana, Calif.: Steve Smith Autosports, 1977. 168 p. Diags. Photos.

Written to help mechanics set up and maintain a competitive stock car, the book covers transmission preparation, setting the rear end, the electrical system, building the chassis and roll cage, welding, clutches, safety systems, fabrication, wheels and tires, and the cooling and plumbing systems, in short--how to build a stocker from the ground up.

_____. THE STOCK CAR RACING CHASSIS: DESIGN/THEORY/ CONSTRUCTION. Santa Ana, Calif.: Steve Smith Autosports, 1972. 26 p.

The basic handling and suspension book for stock car racers and mechanics, it provides useful information on basic racing setups. Topics included are caster, camber, toe-out, tire temperatures, wedge, springs, and sorting a chassis. A special bonus for those wanting to race a Chevelle is a chapter dealing exclusively with this model. Basic principles can be applied to other cars. A revised edition is due soon.

Smith, Steve, and Lamar, Paul. RACE CAR BRAKING SYSTEMS. Rev. ed. Santa Ana, Calif.: Steve Smith Autosports, 1977. 74 p. Diags. Photos.

An in-depth look at the workings of automotive braking systems, this book covers both drum and disc systems. Useful information for racers includes such items as the best fluids to use, which passenger car systems are usable, and how to proportion front to rear bias. Basics of the hydraulics of braking would be useful to anyone, but the book was prepared to aid racers in selection and use of braking components for competition machinery. There is no index. A parts supplier list is included as are parts numbers from the American firms Grey Rock and Bendix.

Terry, Len, and Baker, Alan. RACING CAR DESIGN AND DEVELOPMENT. Cambridge, Mass.: Robert Bentley, 1973. 256 p. Diags. Photos.

Terry and Baker cover virtually every aspect of race car design: handling, aerodynamics, cooling, braking, chassis and suspension, wheels and tires, safety, materials and components, driver comfort, and all the myriad details involved in a race car. Terry is a successful designer; Baker a technical writer; both are engineers. They have produced a thorough, well thought out combination of theory and practical information on modern race car design. The book is relevant to most types of racing except drag racing. A list of suppliers has limited use since most are British.

Thawley, John. PRACTICAL ENGINE SWAPPING. Santa Ana, Calif.: Steve Smith Autosports, 1977. 124 p. Diags. Charts. Photos.

Thawley covers all aspects of engine swapping. Problem areas such as driveline, motor mounts, wiring, exhaust, and linkages are discussed in detail. The charts are particularly helpful in determining the primary question "Will it fit?" It is a useful book for the automotive do-it-yourselfer.

______. RACING THE SMALL BLOCK CHEVY. Santa Ana, Calif.: Steve Smith Autosports, 1977. 152 p. Diags. Photos.

A detailed discussion of the small-block Chevy engine gives many ideas on how to get the most power and reliability from this popular engine. Information provided by Smokey Yunick, Junior Johnson, Waddell Wilson, and others also adds knowledge gained by long experience. All aspects of the engine, such as carburetors, rods, pistons, cranks, heads, valve gear, and blocks are covered. There is no index. A heavy duty parts list is a helpful addition.

THE TRANS AM AND CORVETTE CHASSIS: DESIGN/THEORY/CONSTRUCTION. Santa Ana, Calif.: Steve Smith Autosports, 1975? 30 p. Illus.

This is an advanced book on building up a racing chassis for the

Corvette, Camaro, and Mustang chassis. The primary emphasis is on road racing. Former Chevrolet engineer, driver, and acknowledged chassis expert Dick Guldstrand provided his expertise. Chapters include spring rate selection, roll couple distribution, bump steer, racing tires, weight distribution and transfer, antiroll bars, roll center height, shocks, and roll cages.

Trickey, Clive. RACING ENGINE PREPARATION. Speed Sport Series. New York: British Book Centre, 1973. 74 p. Illus.

Trickey has written a good basic guide to preparing engines for competition. There is a particularly good discussion of engine components and modifications.

Valkenburgh, Paul Van. RACE CAR ENGINEERING AND MECHANICS. New York: Dodd, Mead and Co., 1976. 307 p. Diags. Photos.

A more technical book than the Terry-Baker effort RACING CAR DESIGN AND DEVELOPMENT, Valkenburgh's work is excellent. He covers all areas of race car engineering, theory, development, and mechanics. Some information applies to all types of racing including drag racing. Included are chapters on tires and wheels, suspension geometry and alignment, springs, antiroll bars, shocks, brakes, aerodynamics, handling, engine support systems, gearing, frames, safety, testing, and pit work.

Vizard, David. HOW TO MODIFY YOUR MINI. Tucson, Ariz.: H.P. Books, 1977. 192 p. Paperbound. Photos.

This book covers the engines for Marina 1300, MG Midget, Morris Minor, Austin Healy Sprite, and Austin America among others. Vizard discusses bolt-on performance modifications. All aspects of engine performance are covered.

Waar, Bob. BAJA-PREPARING VW SEDANS AND DUNE BUGGIES. Tucson, Ariz.: H.P. Books, 1970. 96 p. B/w photos.

A book for the hardy soul who wants to desert crowded streets for the unfamiliar hazards of off-road competition, it is very much a "how to" book. Waar's book provides detailed instructions on preparing a VW for off-road racing. Suggestions, optional equipment choices, and plenty of warnings as to what will happen when the basics are disregarded make this a useful book. No index is provided.

Wilson, Waddell, and Smith, Steve. RACING ENGINE PREPARATION. Santa Ana, Calif.: Steve Smith Autosports, 1975. 151 p. Diags. Charts. Photos.

An excellent book for anyone wanting to race stock cars, it is not for shade tree mechanics or amateurs. The person seriously involved in preparing stock car race engines will find it useful. Ignition systems, crankshaft, rods, pistons, valve train, headers, cams, and heads are a few of the topics covered. Wilson's suggestions and comments grew from over twenty years of successful engine building. No index is provided.

Chapter 2
MOTORCYCLE RACING

A. HISTORICAL AND GENERAL

Boulton, Jim, comp. THE FIRST POST-VINTAGE SCENE. Leatherhead, Australia: Bruce Main-Smith and Co., 1976. 64 p. Illus.

This book covers the motorcycle racing scene from 1931 to 1951. There is a companion volume, also published by Bruce Main-Smith and Co., entitled THE FIRST VINTAGE RACING (PRE 1931).

Briggs, Barry. TRACKIN' WITH BRIGGO. Briggo Motorcycle Racing Library, no. 4. London: Souvenir Press, 1975. 128 p. Illus.

Bula, Maurice. GRAND PRIX MOTORCYCLE CHAMPIONSHIPS OF THE WORLD 1949-1975. Yeovil, Engl.: G.T. Foulis, 1975. 300 p. Illus.

This book deals with Grand Prix motorcycle racing.

Carrick, Peter. ENCYCLOPAEDIA OF MOTOR-CYCLE SPORT. New York: St. Martin's Press, 1977. 224 p. Index. B/w photos.

The period covered is from the birth of organized motorcycle racing in the early 1900s to the present. Included are histories of major factories, biographies, and descriptions of important races. Emphasis is on road racing but coverage includes moto-cross, scrambling, trials, grass track, sprinting, drag racing, and world record attempts. Speedway racing is only lightly covered. It is arranged alphabetically. Articles vary in length. Later editions are planned.

______. GREAT MOMENTS IN SPORT: MOTORCYCLE RACING. London: Pelham Books, 1977. 142 p. Index. Photos.

The author discusses some of the most exciting motorcycle races ever run. The emphasis is British.

______. HELL RAISERS. London: Pelham Books, 1973. 173 p. Index. Bibliography.

A fascinating look at motorcycle racing in the 1960s when Japan dominated the sport with Yamaha, Suzuki, and the great Hondas. The story is presented mainly by looking at the great riders of this era--Bill Ivy, John Cooper, Fritz Scheidegger, Derek Minter, and Phil Read among others. There is a short chapter on American riders including Gary Nixon and Evel Knievel, and a chapter on Dave Degens and the ban imposed on him when he went to prison. An appendix lists the winners in all classes from 1960 to 1969, the official world speed records, and the TT races from 1960 to 1969 including year, class, and the top three riders and their machines.

______. THE STORY OF HONDA MOTORCYCLES. Cambridge, Engl.: Patrick Stephens, 1976. 136 p. Index. Illus.

The author covers Honda the man and Honda the machine and describes Honda's road racing triumphs in the 1960s including sixteen world championships and 137 Grand Prix wins.

______, ed. BOOK OF MOTOR CYCLE RACING. Foreword by Phil Read. London: Stanley Paul, 1967. 126 p. Illus.

This is an interesting book on motorcycle racing by an experienced and knowledgeable motorsport journalist.

Clew, Jeff. BRITISH RACING MOTORCYCLES. Yeovil, Engl.: G.T. Foulis, 1976. 183 p. Illus.

This historical work on all road racing British machines covers both famous and obscure makes.

DIRT BIKE, ed. CRASH AND BURN. Encino, Calif.: Hi-Torque Publications, 1977. 74 p. Paperbound.

In magazine format, this is a pictorial essay on motorcycle crashes with tag lines, most of them humorous. No fatalities or serious injuries are covered. There is not much sense to the format, but the fan may enjoy it.

Edmunds, I.G. MOTORCYCLE RACING FOR BEGINNERS. New York: Holt, Rinehart and Winston, 1977. 144 p. Index. Glossary. Illus.

This book covers all types of racing--hillclimb, motocross, desert, national championships, and observed trials. It describes the American Motorcycle Association and its youth division--Y-AMA. Rules, protective clothing, equipment, and bike maintenance are also discussed. It is excellent reading for young riders wanting to get started.

Griffen, Al. MOTORCYCLES: A BUYER'S AND RIDER'S GUIDE. Rev. Chicago: Henry Regnery Co., 1974. 317 p. Index. Illus.

This book covers all motorcycles through 1974 and has chapters on "Competition Bikes," "Desert Bikes," and "Woods Bikes." The author devotes space to the world's record motorcycles and has several appendixes including outlaw motorcycle gangs, world's speed records, piston displacement equivalents, motorcycle publications, and motorcycle manufacturers' distributors.

Griffin, John Q. MOTORCYCLES ON THE MOVE; A BRIEF HISTORY. Minneapolis: Lerner Publications Co., 1976. 51 p. Col. and b/w photos.

Griffin covers the history and development of motorcycles, including information on the growth of motorcycle racing. Motorcycles designed for racing are also discussed in comparison to other types of motorcycles. There is no index.

Griffith, John. FAMOUS RACING MOTORCYCLES. Leatherhead, Australia: Bruce Main-Smith and Co., 1973. 108 p.

The book describes fifty bikes.

Hartley, Peter. BIKES AT BROOKLANDS, IN THE PIONEER YEARS. Norwich, Engl.: Goose and Sons, 1973. 252 p.

This is a history of the early days of motorcycle racing at Brooklands race track in Weybridge, England.

Holliday, Bob. THE STORY OF BSA MOTORCYCLES. Newfoundland, N.J.: Haessner, 1978. 128 p. Drwgs., photos.

Holliday tells the story of the competition history of BSA along with a description of the road-going bikes. Some of BSA's more notable triumphs at Brooklands, in the TT, at Daytona Beach, in the Six Day Trials, in marathons, on speedways, and in motocross are recounted here. An interesting book on a famous British motorcycle.

Hough, Richard, and Setright, L.J.K. A HISTORY OF THE WORLD'S MOTORCYCLES. New York: Harper and Row, 1966. 192 p. Photos.

A history of motorcycle development with emphasis on racing, the book is thorough and well done. Some of the most exciting events and personalities are included. Developments in the technical field are especially interesting.

Houlgate, Deke. THE COMPLETE MOTORCYCLE BOOK. New York: Four Winds Press, 1974. 195 p. Index. Illus.

Produced by Lyle Kenyon Engel, this book covers all aspects of cycling with a definite emphasis on racing. Road racing, dirt racing, trials, off-road competition, and drag racing are all discussed. Early motorcycle racing is briefly mentioned. Trick and stunt riding is also included in an interesting chapter entitled "Flagpole Sitting on a Bike."

Lacombe, Christian. THE MOTORCYCLE. New York: Grosset and Dunlap, 1974. 231 p. Diags. B/w photos.

Lacombe covers all aspects of motorcycling with heavy emphasis on racing. Beautifully illustrated with photos and excellent diagrams, the book is a visual delight. The history and development of the motorcycle, riding tips, and technical descriptions of modern motorcycle design are included.

McIntyre, Bob. MOTOR CYCLING TODAY. London: Arthur Barker, 1962. 128 p.

Bob McIntyre, an exciting rider at his peak in the 1950s and early sixties, talks about motorcycling as he sees it. McIntyre was also well known for his success in the TT.

Nicks, Mike. MOTORCYCLE RACING MANUAL. London: Patrick Stephens, 1973. 120 p. Illus.

Nicks covers all aspects of motorcycle racing. Contributions to this book were made by ten top experts in road racing. The title on the spine is CASTROL MOTORCYCLE RACING MANUAL.

Puleo, Nicole. MOTORCYCLE RACING. Fearon Racing Series. Belmont, Calif.: published for Lear Siegler by Fearon Publishers, 1974. 47 p. Col. photos.

Simply written, this book provides coverage of various types of motorcycle racing events as well as historical background. Enduro, cross-country, road, and dirt track racing, hill climbing, and drag racing are all included. The book was written especially for slower readers.

Renstrom, Richard C. GREAT MOTORCYCLE LEGENDS. Newfoundland, N.J.: Haessner, 1977. 128 p. B/w photos.

First published in 1972 under the title THE GREAT MOTORCYCLES, the book covers the history of twenty-two of the most important marques in motorcycle sports. The competition history of each is featured.

Scalzo, Joe. THE MOTORCYCLE BOOK. Englewood Cliffs, N.J.: Prentice-Hall, 1974. 210 p. Index. Col. and b/w photos.

Scalzo covers all aspects of motorcycling as a sport. The first part of the book is devoted to the basics--a brief history, easy maintenance, and the various categories of bikes. The other four parts are devoted to motorcycle competition in one form or another. Included are off-road riding, dirt track racing, road racing, motocross, hill climbing, indoor racing, sidecar racing, the speed records, and stunt riding. One chapter is devoted exclusively to women racers.

Schilling, Phil. THE MOTORCYCLE WORLD. New York: Ridge Press Books, 1974. 252 p. Index. Illus.

This is a general work on the past and present of motorcycling including, as part of its panorama, the world of cycle racing. Covered are a historical view of the Isle of Man plus the entrance of German, Japanese, and American bikes and riders on the racing scene. Material on off-road racing, motocross, and Australian rider Kel Carruthers is also included.

Schneiders, Ron. ISDT '73: THE OLYMPICS OF MOTORCYCLING: THE OFFICIAL PICTORIAL RECORD OF THE 48TH INTERNATIONAL SIX DAYS TRIAL, PITTSFIELD, MASS. U.S.A. Radnor, Pa.: Chilton Book Co., 1973. 156 p. Appendix. Col. and b/w photos.

This is a pictorial record of the International Six Days Trial held in the United States in 1973. The text complements the photographs well. The paper is of excellent quality and the book is intended to be a permanent record of the event. A section on the rules and one on scoring prove essential to understanding the complicated proceedings. An appendix provides complete results with a list of the teams and small photos of each rider. This is excellent coverage of a major motorcycle event.

Seaver, David-Linn. MINI-BIKE RACING. Philadelphia: J.B. Lippincott, 1972. 32 p. Photos.

Seaver discusses minibikes and how to race them, what is involved in the sport, and how to get started. Photography was done by the author who aimed at a younger audience, that is, from grade nine and up.

Setright, L.J.K. MOTORCYCLES. Preface by Barry Sheene. London: Weidenfeld and Nicolson, 1976. 159 p. Index. Illus.

The author describes twenty-four classic machines including roadsters and racers.

Spence, James, and Brown, Gar. MOTORCYCLE RACING IN AMERICA: A DEFINITIVE LOOK AT THE SPORT. Chicago: J. Philip O'Hara, 1974. 134 p. B/w photos.

This might be termed an introductory reference manual to motorcycle racing. The book is broken down into nine types of racing--oval track, road racing, motocross, speedway/Class A, desert racing, observed trials, tourist trophy, hillclimb, and enduro (International Six-Days Trial). Within each chapter there is an orderly presentation of history, equipment used, apparel, the courses, competition format, rider classification, the national championship, and a description of a typical race. An informative gold mine, this well-done, highly recommended book is one no racing collection can afford to be without.

Swift, Jim. RIDE IT! THE COMPLETE BOOK OF BIG BIKE RACING. Yeovil, Engl.: G.T. Foulis, 1976. 149 p. Illus.

This book covers big bike competition with a European emphasis.

Willoughby, Vic. CLASSIC MOTORCYCLES. New York: Dial Press, 1975. 176 p. Drwgs., photos.

The author ranges over sixty years of cycles covering forty machines including some racing bikes.

Wise, David Burgess. HISTORIC MOTOR CYCLES. London: Hamlyn, 1973. 96 p. Index.

This history discusses motorcycle development from the beginning when they ran on steam to the 1970s. Wise covers the start of cycle racing, the TT races, the cyclecar, cycling in the Jazz Age, the use of cycles in military service, and the effect of the depression on the motorcycle industry.

Wood, Geoffrey, and Renstrom, Richard C. THE GREAT MOTORCYCLES: HISTORIES OF 22 FAMOUS MAKES. Newport Beach, Calif.: Bond/Parkhurst Publications, 1972. 120 p. Illus.

A separate chapter is devoted to each make including its competition history. Bikes covered are AJS, Ariel, BMW, BSA, Bultaco, Ducati, Greeves, Honda, Husqvarna, Jawa, Lambretta, Matchless, Montesa, Moto Gilera, Moto Guzzi, Norton, NSU, Ossa, Puch, Royal Enfield, Triumph, and Velocette. This book is well done.

Woollett, Mick. RACING MOTORCYCLES. London: Hamlyn, 1973. 96 p. Index. Illus.

This is a history of motorcycle racing which does not bog down in dull detail but skims the surface in a refreshing interest-generating style. Woollett covers the first efforts of racing, proceeds into the postwar revival, describes the triumph and fading of the Japanese machines, and ends with a glance at the American scene.

B. SPEEDWAY

Lanning, David. SPEEDWAY AND SHORT TRACK RACING. London: Hamlyn, 1974. 128 p. Index. Photos.

Devoted mostly to European speedway motorcycle racing, the book begins with a brief history beginning in Australia in the 1920s and then goes into a series of brief biographies of such racers as Zenon Plech of Poland, Peter Collins of England, Johnny Boulger of Australia, and Barry Briggs of New Zealand. The coverage is superficial.

Louis, John. A SECOND LOOK INSIDE SPEEDWAY. Ipswich, Engl.: Studio Publications, 1976. 144 p. Illus.

Broad coverage of speedway cycle racing includes the events themselves, the men, and the mechanical developments.

Mauger, Ivan, and Oakes, Peter, eds. IVAN MAUGER'S SPEEDWAY EXTRAVAGANZA NO. 1. Ipswich, Engl.: Studio Publications, 1975. 112 p. Illus.

This general collection of cycle-racing feature articles include a biography of American Mike Bast and a piece on the ten greatest riders of all time.

______. IVAN MAUGER'S SPEEDWAY EXTRAVAGANZA NO. 2. Ipswich, Engl.: Studio Publications, 1976. 112 p.

This second collection of feature articles on cycle racing includes a "Fan Club Guide" with facts about leading racers.

______. IVAN MAUGER'S SPEEDWAY SPECTACULAR. London: Pelham Books, 1975. 136 p. B/w photos.

Another of Ivan Mauger's fine collections of articles written on the sport of speedway, there are several pieces on individual riders including Jerzy Szczakiel of Poland, Geoff Mardon of New Zealand, and Steve Reinke of Australia. Also of interest are the chapters on speedway in New Guinea and speedway racing on the ice. Much information is found here that is not available in other books.

______. IVAN MAUGER'S WORLD SPEEDWAY BOOK. London: Pelham Books, 1973. 120 p. B/w photos.

This is a collection of articles on speedway motorcycle racing. Two of the articles focus on Ivan Mauger himself--one of the stars of speedway--but most of the other pieces are on speedway and its development as well as current stars and status in other countries besides England. Covered are Japan, Poland, the United States, New Zealand, Australia, Sweden, and Rhodesia. The photographs are mostly portrait shots of current racers. It is a well-done book.

May, Cyril. RIDE IT! THE COMPLETE BOOK OF SPEEDWAY. Yeovil, Engl.: G.T. Foulis, 1976. 156 p. Illus.

May covers speedway racing primarily in England.

Patrick, Mike. FOCUS ON SPEEDWAY. Text by Martin Rogers. Ipswich, Engl.: Studio Publications, 1975. 96 p. Photos.

Fifty spectacular action pictures that chronicle the world champion motorcyclists and national champions.

C. TRIALS

Jones, Thomas Firth. ENDURO. Philadelphia: Chilton Book Co., 1970. 155 p.

An excellent guide to the wonders of the enduro, this book includes sections on how to buy and modify a motorcycle, what to wear and carry during the competition, and tips on correct riding technique. The final chapters explain the procedures for organizing and laying out a proper competition.

King, Max. MOTOR-CYCLE TRIALS RIDING. Foreword by Gordon Farby and a special contribution by Mick Andrews. 4th ed., rev. London: Pelham Books, 1972. 192 p. Illus.

This is a good book on the "how-to" of trials riding.

Miller, Sammy. SAMMY MILLER ON TRIAL. 2d ed. Newport Beach, Calif.: Bond, Parkhurst Publications, 1971. 112 p. B/w photos.

This good introductory text written by a champion rider leads the reader step-by-step from instructions for the beginner, through the purchase of the necessary machinery and its preparations, the transport needed, the clothing and tools required, and the advisable degree of physical fitness. Then Miller gets down to the basics of the trials themselves explaining the different sections along with instructions on how to ride them. There are explanations of special tests used to decide a position in the event of two riders having the same marks and a chapter on the International Six Day Trials. Trial Bike Specifications are included.

Perry, Robin. THE TRIALS MOTORCYCLIST: HOW TO BUY, EQUIP, AND

RIDE YOUR BIKE IN OBSERVED TRIALS. New York: Crown Publishers, 1975. 152 p.

This is a comprehensive guide to observed trials and what a motorcyclist needs to know in order to compete successfully. Perry covers the bike, maintenance, riding techniques, and buying hints.

_____. THE WOODS RIDER: A GUIDE TO OFF-THE-ROAD MOTORCYCLING. New York: Crown Publishers, 1973. 144 p. B/w photos.

Perry provides an excellent easy-to-read introduction to off-road motorcycling. Different techniques such as fording a stream, riding on sand or ice, and jumping and hill climbing are explained.

Sanford, Bob. RIDING THE DIRT. Newport Beach, Calif.: Bond, Parkhurst Publications, 1972. 221 p. Glossary. B/w photos.

An instructional introduction to motorcycle dirt riding, Sanford covers techniques beneficial to both the novice and more experienced rider. Specific topics covered include preparing and maintaining a trail bike, motocrosses, and enduros.

Shipman, Carl. HOW TO RIDE OBSERVED TRIALS. New York: H.P. Publishing Co., 1973. 158 p. Illus.

Shipman covers riding techniques, modifying your cycle, how to start a club, and provides sample forms and charts.

Smith, Don. RIDE IT! THE COMPLETE BOOK OF MOTORCYCLE TRIALS. Yeovil, Engl.: G.T. Foulis, 1975. 133 p. Illus.

This work covers all aspects of trials competition.

D. MOTORCROSS

Bailey, Gary, with Shipman, Carl. HOW TO WIN MOTOCROSS. Tucson, Ariz.: H.P. Books, 1974. 190 p. B/w photos.

This well-done complete guide to motocross by a man who teaches the sport leaves no detail to the imagination. He covers equipment, setting up a bike for racing, riding techniques, getting a bike to the track, and racing technique. The photos are an essential part of the instruction and very informative.

Davis, Jim, and Jackson, Bob. THE COMPLETE BOOK OF MOTO-CROSS. Lake Arrowhead, Calif.: Bagnall Publishing Co., 1972. 112 p. Photos.

This book includes the basics of motocross, what it is, how to start, what to wear, how to prepare your bike, techniques, and strategy.

Melling, Frank. THE COMPLETE BOOK OF MOTOCROSS. Yeovil, Engl.: G.T. Foulis, 1975. 157 p. Illus.

This book covers most aspects of the sport of motocross.

Seaver, David-Linn. MOTO-CROSS RACING. Philadelphia: J.B. Lippincott, 1972. 32 p. Photos.

Both the writing and photography were done by Seaver. He discusses motocross, the bikes, the men, and the rules. It's aimed at a younger audience, grade nine and up.

E. TOURIST TROPHY

Arnold, Peter. TT RACES: DIAMOND JUBILEE 1907-1967. London: Shell-Mex and BP Ltd. 192 p. Illus.

Arnold details the history of the Isle of Man Tourist Trophy races. This event has long been considered one of the most important and prestigious events in cycle competition. This is an interesting account of an incredible race.

Deane, Charles. ISLE OF MAN TT. Cambridge, Engl.: Patrick Stephens, 1975. 152 p. Illus.

This history of the famed thirty-seven-and-three-quarter-mile motorcycle races begins in 1907 and continues through the first thirty years, the postwar races, and the Japanese bikes. There is a biographical chapter on the all-time great riders.

Holliday, Bob, and Keig, S.R. THE KEIG COLLECTION. 3 vols. Leatherhead, Australia: Bruce Main-Smith and Co., 1975-- . Photos. by Stanley Robertson Keig.

This series contains six hundred photographs of TT riders and their machines from 1911 to 1939 from the Manx house of Keig.

Mutch, Ronnie. THE LAST OF THE GREAT ROAD RACES: THE ISLE OF MAN TT. London: Transport, 1975. 135 p. Illus.

This historical look at the men who have ridden the Isle of Man TT from its beginning till today provides good coverage of the race itself.

F. BIOGRAPHY

Butcher, Grace. MOTORCYCLING. Women in Sports series. New York: Harvey House, 1976. 62 p.

Butcher briefly recounts the careers of eight women who are successful motorcycle racers.

Clew, Jeff. SAMMY MILLER: THE WILL TO WIN. Yeovil, Engl.: G.T. Foulis, 1976. 165 p.

The biography of world famous trials rider Sammy Miller goes from his days as a schoolboy push-bike "whizz kid" through his eleven successive British Championship titles.

Hailwood, Mike, and Macauley, Ted. HAILWOOD. London: Cassell, 1968. 118 p. Illus.

This biography of wealthy bike rider Mike Hailwood covers his twelve TT wins and nine world championships.

Mann, Dick, with Scalzo, Joe. MOTORCYCLE ACE. Chicago: Henry Regnery Co., 1972. 198 p.

This is a biography of a man who has raced motorcycles for over twenty years and emerged as a champion. It traces Mann's life from his days playing football in Richmond, California, to his adventures with motorcycle and racing driver Joe Leonard, his battles with the American Motorcycle Association, and his hard racing with ace Gene Romero. It's a good look at what it takes to race motorcycles.

Minter, Derek. RACING ALL MY LIFE. London: Arthur Barker, 1965. 96 p. Illus.

Minter was a popular rider and enjoyed some success on a variety of bikes, but, like many riders, he was also controversial. Minter was not afraid to say what he thought and his book is no different, which makes it interesting reading. Minter retired from active competition in October 1967, after a race at Brands Hatch, so he was still racing when this book was written.

Peck, Alan. NO TIME TO LOSE: THE FAST MOVING WORLD OF BILL IVY. Croyden, Engl.: Motor Racing Publications, 1972. 160 p.

This is a biography of Bill Ivy, one of the most dynamic stars of motorcycle racing in the 60s. Ivy was killed in practice for the East German Grand Prix in 1969. Peck's biography was written after Ivy's death and reveals a complex man with a great deal of charisma. Peck's analysis of Ivy's final accident provides additional information.

Redman, Jim. WHEELS OF FORTUNE. London: Stanley Paul, 1966. 123 p.

Jim Redman, a highly successful rider in the decade of the 1960s, talks about his life and career in motorcycle racing.

Saltman, Sheldon, and Green, Maury. EVEL KNIEVEL ON TOUR. New York: Dell Publishing Co., 1977. 208 p. Paperbound.

A candid look at the daredevil motorcycle ace which doesn't hesitate to cover both pleasant and unpleasant aspects of his character, this paperback is centered around the hoopla and background of his famed Snake River Canyon jump.

Scalzo, Joe. THE BART MARKEL STORY. Newport Beach, Calif.: Bond, Parkhurst Publications, 1972. 125 p. Illus.

This biography of motorcycle racing champion Bart Markel, by a noted racing writer, is an interesting look at Markel's career and the trials and tribulations of motorcycle racers.

_____. RACER: THE STORY OF GARY NIXON. Newport Beach, Calif.: Bond, Parkhurst Publications, 1970. 92 p. Illus.

This biography of motorcycle ace Gary Nixon details Nixon's successful career.

Spiegel, Marshall. THE CYCLE JUMPERS. New York: Scholastic Book Services, 1973. 174 p. B/w photos.

These biographies of two people--one a man, one a mere boy, who jump motorcycles--are interesting reading. The book is about evenly divided as to material on Evel Knievel and to an upcoming jumper called Gary Wells. The material is presented in an interesting style with an abundance of quotes. More than library research went into this book as Spiegel went out and talked with his subjects and it shows.

Whyte, Norrie, ed. MOTORCYCLE RACING CHAMPIONS. New York: Arco Publishing Co., 1976. 96p. Illus.

Here is the real action from the world's motorcycling scene, captured by MOTOR CYCLE NEWS' globe-trotting team of photographers and reporters.

G. RACING TECHNOLOGY

Irving, P.E. TUNING FOR SPEED: HOW TO INCREASE THE PERFORMANCE

OF ANY MOTORCYCLE ENGINE FOR RACING AND COMPETITION WORK. 5th ed. New York: Hamlyn, 1969. 248 p. Index. Appendix.

This is a book only for the skilled motorcycle mechanic who is interested in fashioning a competition racing engine. The book is highly technical covering such topics as carburetion, compression ratios, fuels, pistons and rings, flywheels, valves, superchargers, and many more. An appendix provides many useful tables and formulas including a fuel analysis table. This is a very good book of its kind.

Knight, Ray. RACING AND TUNING PRODUCTION MOTORBIKES. London: Speed and Sports Publications, 1970. 123 p. Illus.

Basic information on competing successfully with a production model is given. Tips on how to obtain the most from a bike and ideas on competition setups are given.

Shipman, Carl. MOTORCYCLE TUNING FOR PERFORMANCE. 2d ed. Tucson, Ariz.: H.P. Books, 1973. 174 p. Index. Diags. Charts. Tables. Photos.

Shipman covers basic tuning for high performance machinery. Topics discussed are engine timing, carburetion, ignition, engine modifications, performance measurements, and record keeping. Material is useful for all types of high performance bikes especially dirt bikes and drag bikes.

Chapter 3
Motorsports—Recreational

A. RALLYING

Anderson, Eric, ed. PERFORMANCE RALLYING. Modern Sports Car Series. New York: Sports Car Press, 1975. 117 p. Illus. Paperbound.

> Anderson discusses car preparation, driving, and navigating techniques and how to get started in high performance rallying. This is a type of rallying which differs from the usual time, speed, and distance rallying. Chapter authors are all experienced high performance rallyists.

Brittan, Nick. SAFARI FEVER: THE STORY OF A CAR RALLY THEY SAID NO EUROPEAN COULD WIN. Croydon, Engl.: Motor Racing Publications, 1972. 208 p. Photos.

> The author covers the 1972 East African Safari, one of the toughest rallies run. The Ford team of Mikkola and Palm surprised a lot of people who said no European team could ever win. Brittan follows the adventures of this team throughout the event while providing some history and background on the safari for 1953. John Davenport provided additional information.

Browing, Peter, ed. CASTROL RALLY MANUAL 2. Minneapolis: Motorbooks International, 1972. 128 p. Photos.

> Not a revision of the first Castrol Rally Manual, this is a new collection of articles and reference material for rally drivers, navigators, organizers, and enthusiasts. Interesting and informative, these articles on tires, servicing, East African events, updated specifications, and addresses are very helpful.

Calvin, Jean. RALLYING TO WIN: A COMPLETE GUIDE TO NORTH AMERICAN RALLYING. Newport Beach, Calif.: Bond, Parkhurst Publications, 1974. 174 p.

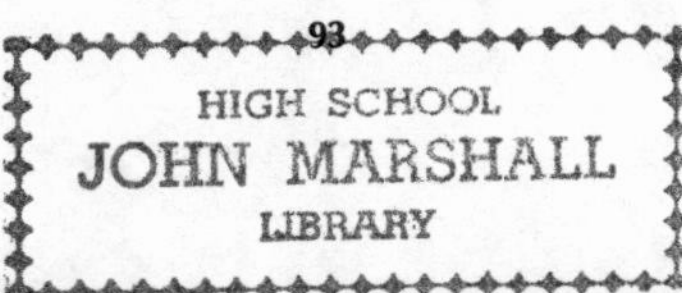

Jean Calvin is a well-known rallyist who has written an excellent guide to the sport. While acting as a tutor for the uninitiated, she has also compiled a gold mine of information for the pro. Unafraid of detail, she has reached beneath the surface of rallying and brought to the fore all the tiny tips that make the difference between a winner and a DNF. Especially entertaining is the section on gimmick rallies, which describes a poker run, treasure hunt, photo rally, and the famous airchair rally--the St. Valentine's Day Massacre.

Clark, Roger, in collaboration with Graham Robson. SIDEWAYS TO VICTORY. Croydon, Engl.: Motor Racing Publications, 1976. 256 p. Illus.

British rally champion Roger Clark tells his story of his climb to the top of the rally heap. Clark can take on and beat the nearly invincible Scandinavians and his experiences are interesting and encouraging to any competitive driver.

Davenport, John. RALLY. London: Hamlyn, 1977. 159 p. Index. Illus.

This excellent book deals with international class rallying. Davenport is the competition manager for British Leyland in the United Kingdom and has the experience and background to write this primer of the sport. He covers the competition from its origins through armchair rallying to the World Cup Marathon.

Drackett, Phil. RALLY OF THE FORESTS: THE STORY OF RAC INTERNATIONAL RALLY OF GREAT BRITAIN. London: Pelham Books, 1970. 170 p. Index. Illus.

This is an account of one of England's most exciting and challenging rallies.

Greasley, Mike, ed. CASTROL RALLY MANUAL 3. Minneapolis: Motorbooks International, 1974. 128 p. Appendixes. Photos.

Another interesting collection of rally materials for all rally buffs, the articles cover stage events, maps and navigating, rule bending, and sponsorship. There are useful appendixes containing names and addresses, results, and championships.

Green, Evan. A BOOT FULL OF RIGHT ARMS: ADVENTURE IN THE LONDON-SAHARA-MUNICH WORLD CUP RALLY AND OTHER MOTORING MARATHONS. Stanmore, N.S.W.: Cassell Australia, 1975. 281 p. Maps. Illus.

An interesting and readable story of the London-Sahara-Munich World Cup Rally, the reader travels through fourteen countries and over some of the most challenging terrain in the world. One car managed to finish the 17,000 kilometers. Green also mentions earlier rallies and some of the drivers who competed in them.

Hammond, Gene. THE SPORTS CAR RALLY HANDBOOK. Rev. New York: Sterling Publishing Co., 1962. 144 p.

A comprehensive text on rallying, this book covers duties of driver and navigator, use of clocks, calculators, maps and odometers, math for experts and amateurs, scoring, checkpoint procedure, and general tips on following instructions and getting back on course.

Hebb, David. THE RALLY BOOK. New York: Hawthorn Books, 1973. 176 p.

An excellent guide to rallying which is a delight to novice and expert alike. Hebb provides complete chapters on how to interpret general instructions and follow a route. Anyone who has ever been lost due to the wily tricks of a rally master will recognize the helpful hints Hebb drops. There is also material on exotic equipment and clothes for rallying, and precise instructions on how to set up your own rally course.

Hebb, David, and Peck, Arthur. SPORTS CAR RALLIES, TRIALS AND GYMKHANAS. Great Neck, N.Y.: Channel Press, 1960. 159 p. Tables.

A well-presented basic approach to a fun oriented part of a sports car club--rallying, this is a good book for a beginner either as a participant or as an organizer. Besides covering the obvious odometer usage, speed calculations, and map reading, the book presents many gimmick ideas such as a Halloween rally, poker rally, or a compass rally. Gymkhanas and trials are also covered. TSD tables are included.

Holmes, Martin. RALLY NAVIGATION. Minneapolis: Motorbooks International, 1977. 156 p. Illus.

Holmes gives a vast amount of information for codrivers in performance rallies. Holmes is an experienced navigator and his discussion of road rallies, stage rallies, map reading, pace notes, service crew organization, route cards, time cards, and preparation is very valuable. This would be a good companion volume to PERFORMANCE RALLYING by Eric Anderson.

Hudson-Evans, Richard. THE RALLY HANDBOOK. Minneapolis: Motorbooks International, 1972. 206 p. Appendixes.

Hudson-Evans starts from the very beginning and provides all the details one needs to know to enter any class of international rallying. The book touches on licensing, insurance, clothing, preparation, tires, and how-to-do-it. The appendixes listing information sources and suppliers make a very useful book.

Hudson-Evans, Richard, and Robson, Graham. THE BIG DRIVE: THE BOOK OF THE WORLD CUP RALLY, 1970. Elmford, N.Y.: British Book Centre, 1971. 72 p.

The 1970 World Cup Rally covered 16,000 miles, started in London and ended in Mexico City. It was one of the biggest and toughest rallies ever run. Hudson-Evans, a competitor, and Robson, the marshall, tell the story of this epic adventure. Ninety-six cars began the event and only twenty-three finished. From this description of the event and the hazards the teams faced, it seems remarkable that anyone finished.

Ireland, Innes. SIDEWAYS TO SYDNEY: DRIVING LIKE A LUNATIC ACROSS EUROPE, ASIA, AND AUSTRALIA. New York: William Morrow and Co., 1970. 208 p.

The funny, frantic, informative tale of the London to Sydney Marathon as driven by Innes Ireland, Michael Taylor, and Andrew Hedges was published in England under the title MARATHON IN THE DUST.

Malkin, Colin. HOW TO START RALLYING. Newfoundland, N.J.: Haessner, 1973. 98 p. Illus.

Malkin, a successful British rally competitor discusses international rallying and how to prepare a car for competition. Some of the topics covered are choosing a car, setting it up, underbody protection, lights, driving techniques, and navigation.

Moss, Pat, and Carlsson, Erik. THE ART AND TECHNIQUE OF DRIVING. London: Heinemann, 1965. 192 p. Illus.

Pat Moss, sister of Stirling Moss, and Erik Carlsson, two of the world's top rally drivers, have teamed up to explain some of the fine points of fast driving and rally techniques.

Palm, Gunnar, and Volker, Herbert. TRICKS OF THE RALLY GAME. Translated from the German by Charles Meisl. London: Ian Allan, 1971. 160 p. Illus.

The authors provide some good firsthand accounts of great rallies, and some insight into the work and effort of the world's leading rally drivers. They also describe some of the techniques utilized by top-flight competition drivers. This book is interesting and informative.

Reid, Larry. LARRY REID'S NEW RALLY TABLES. New York: Sports Car

Press, 1971. 128 p.

Reid presents an easy, workable, inexpensive system for contending with the average speed problem of beginning rallyists or for those who choose not to purchase expensive electronic gear. The tables provide an answer, or a way of finding it, to almost every average speed problem most rallyists will ever encounter in a normal rally. The book is composed of six tables with explanations on how to use them. Table 6, the rally navigation table, is the most extensive and is very helpful, especially for novices.

_____. A NEW GUIDE TO RALLYING. New York: Sports Car Press, 1969. 127 p.

An uncomplicated introduction to the world of rallying, attention is paid to following a rally route, measuring distance with an odometer, calculating average speeds, and organizing and scoring your own rally. A separate chapter is devoted to rally computers. A fine book for beginners, it is very well done.

Reynolds, Roy P., and Clark, Kenneth R. SIXTY MILES OF PENCIL: AN INTIMATE IMPRESSION OF THE BRIGHTON RUN. Foreword by Lord Montagu of Beaulieu. Minneapolis: Motorbooks International, 1971. 126 p. Drwgs.

The authors tell the story of England's Brighton Run, an event held annually for cars built in 1904 or before. Each car is discussed and an illustration provided. A large-sized book, it is very well done and covers an unusual event. The drawings are done by Reynolds and are very good.

Sclater, Chris, and Holmes, Martin. RALLYING: A PRACTICAL GUIDE TO SUCCESSFUL COMPETITION. London: Faber and Faber, 1977. 127 p.

This is a good practical introduction to performance rallying written by an experienced rally driver and navigator. Each man has written six of the twelve chapters concentrating on his particular area of expertise. Sclater covers driving techniques, practicing, tire selection, service crews, and the finding of sponsors. Holmes provides some basic navigation procedure and some advice such as getting plenty of sleep, carrying an alarm clock, and checking and double checking all results. The book is a readable and useful guide to performance rallying.

Stimson, Mike. STIMSON'S RALLY FACTORS. New York: Sports Car Press, 1970. 128 p. Tables.

An extremely useful book for any rallyist, Stimson presents a set of corrected rally navigation factors. The format is useful to both the novice and the seasoned competitor. Topics covered include odometer correction factors, navigational computations, rallying with corrected tables, and 201 tables of minutes-per-mile factors.

Turner, Stuart. INTERNATIONAL RALLYING. Yeovil, Engl.: G.T. Foulis, 1965. 164 p.

Turner discusses the International Rally, one of the longest and toughest in the world. His work is informative and interesting.

_____. RALLYING: PREPARATION, NAVIGATION AND ORGANIZATION. Minneapolis: Motorbooks International, 1971. 119 p.

A top-flight rally navigator, Turner has written a basic guide to rallying, full of helpful hints on navigation and instructions for preparing the car as well as organizing the rally effort. This is very useful for beginning rallyists, but even the more experienced competitor will find it interesting.

B. ALL TERRAIN VEHICLES

Helmker, Judith A. ALL-TERRAIN VEHICLES. New York: A.S. Barnes and Co., 1974. 189 p. Index. B/w photos.

One of the more comprehensive guides to all-terrain vehicles, Helmker covers the development of ATV, rallies, racing, safaris, and driving tips as well as ethics, liability, and ecological implications. The chapters on rallies offer sample courses and give hints on how to organize as well as the rules established by NATVA for racing rallies.

Malo, John. ALL TERRAIN ADVENTURE VEHICLES. New York: Macmillan Co., 1972. 166 p.

Malo discusses one of the fastest growing sports since skiing. ATVs covered include dune buggies, dune scooters, swamp buggies, trail bikes, snowmobiles, minibikes, and three-wheel bikes. Much general information is provided but one useful chapter tells how to use an ATV without damaging the environment.

OFF-ROAD FUN CARS. Los Angeles: Petersen Publishing Co., 1970. 192 p.

This is a collection of articles and pictures on the building of off-road vehicles and how to compete with them. Individual chapters include four-wheelers, driving off-road, tires, races and events, wiring a buggy, and suspensions. It finishes with a catalog of buggies and a directory of manufacturers and suppliers.

C. AUTOCROSS

Carrick, Peter. ALL HELL AND AUTOCROSS . . . MORE HELL AND RALLYCROSS. London: Pelham Books, 1971. 160 p. Index. Appendixes.

A competently presented work, this discusses a sport that is not well covered in auto competition literature. Carrick begins with a history of autocross and rallycross and proceeds into short biographies and glimpses of the men and machines that make the sport possible. Longer biographies are presented for John Bevan--autocross champion, and Peter Harper--rallycross champion. There is a separate chapter on clubs, competition, and sponsorships and a chapter instructing the novice who wants to get a start. This is a good introductory book. Appendix I lists rallycross results for 1970-71. Appendix II lists RAC recognized clubs.

Noad, Peter. HOW TO START AUTOCROSS AND RALLYCROSS. London: Speedsport, 1970. 80 p.

A guide to getting started in autocross and rallycross, areas of motorsport that are rapidly gaining in popularity, this is useful for the newcomer.

Pagel, Jim. HOW TO WIN AT SLALOM AND AUTOCROSS. Modern Sports Car Series. New York: Sports Car Press, 1972. 110 p.

An informative guide to a sometimes press-neglected sports car competition--the slalom, this book gives specific instructions for setting up a club event. Types of cars that normally run slaloms are described along with hints for setting the cars up correctly. A chapter is devoted to the drivers and there is a description of a typical slalom.

Turner, Dick, and Miles, J.B. WINNING AUTOCROSS/SOLO II COMPETITION. Lancaster, Tex.: National Academy for Police Driving, 1977. 128 p. Illus.

This is a useful "how to" volume for Solo II competitors. It begins with a discussion on proper body placement and handling a car. Suspension, acceleration, braking, and cornering are discussed. There is a unique chapter on conditioned reflex autocrossing and the closed loop system. The illustrations are well done and supplement the text.

Chapter 4
LAND SPEED RECORDS

Breedlove, Craig, with Neely, Bill. SPIRIT OF AMERICA: WINNING THE WORLD'S LAND SPEED RECORD. Chicago: Henry Regnery, 1971. 218 p.

This biography of a man who drove a race car at 600 mph and four times set the world's land speed record is interesting reading. In the telling of his story the reader also meets Donald Campbell, Art and Walt Arfons, and Breedlove's former wife, Lee, who set the women's land speed record in her husband's "Spirit of America."

Clifton, Paul. THE FASTEST MEN ON EARTH. New York: John Day Co., 1966. 250 p.

The author tells of the many attempts--both successes and failures--to break the World Land Speed Record. Specifications of each car discussed are given including country of origin, engine, transmission, steering, wheels, tires, weight, and dimensions. Well-known drivers covered include Sir Malcolm Campbell, Donald Campbell, Art Arfons, and Craig Breedlove.

Gregory, Stephen. RACING TO WIN: THE SALT FLATS. Mahwah, N.J.: Troll Associates, 1976. 32 p. Illus.

Gregory discusses the cars and drivers who run against the clock in attempts to set new land speed records at the Bonneville Speedway on the salt flats in Utah. This book is aimed at a younger audience.

Houlgate, Deke. THE FASTEST MEN IN THE WORLD--ON WHEELS. New York: World Publishing, 1971. 164 p. B/w photos.

This is one of the better entries in the land speed sweepstakes. Houlgate, aided by the editors of AUTO RACING MAGAZINE, has fleshed out the telling of the attempts on the land speed records and come up with a readable history that is full of entertaining episodes. He has covered both automobile and motorcycle attempts, and discussed closed course as well as salt flat runs. There is a chart entitled the "Evolution of the Land Speed Record and the Motorcycle Land Speed Record" at the end of the book.

Jackson, Robert B. CARS AGAINST THE CLOCK: THE WORLD LAND SPEED RECORD. New York: Henry Z. Walck, 1971. 64 p.

Jackson gives an extremely simple presentation of the history of the Land Speed Record from its beginnings till the time of Arfons, Breedlove, and Gabelich. Specific attention is paid to electric cars, Henry Ford and the "Arrow," Fred Marriott and the Stanley Bug, and Sir Malcolm Campbell and his son Donald.

Knowles, Arthur, and Campbell, Lady Dorothy. DONALD CAMPBELL C.B.E. South Brunswick, Nova Scotia: A.S. Barnes and Co., 1970. 134 p. Photos.

This is a biography of Sir Donald Campbell, the speed record holder. Campbell's record runs on both land and water are legendary.

Posthumus, Cyril. LAND SPEED RECORD. New York: Crown Publishers, 1971. 256 p. Col. drwgs., b/w photos.

Posthumus gives a history of the land speed record from the first record established by Gaston de Chasseloup-Laubat in 1898 to that set by Gary Gabelich in 1970.

Ross, Frank Jr. CAR RACING AGAINST THE CLOCK: THE STORY OF THE WORLD LAND SPEED RECORD. New York: Lothrop, Lee and Shepard Co., 1976. 128 p. Index. B/w photos.

Ross's book is no better or worse than most of the others written on the Land Speed Record. He covers both the American and British attempts and the familiar names of Campbell, Breedlove, Arfons, and Gabelich. The Appendix is a chronology of world land speed records including the date, driver, car, and place.

Shapiro, Harvey. FASTER THAN SOUND. New York: A.S. Barnes and Co., 1975. 176 p. Index. Bibliography.

Harvey Shapiro has come up with an entry that is readable and contains a unique set of photographs. The usual portraits of the Campbells, Arfons, Thompson, Breedlove, and Gabelich are here and the information for the most part is not new. However, the fan will find this book one of the better ones on the subject.

Stambler, Irwin. THE SUPERCARS AND THE MEN WHO RACE THEM. New York: G.P. Putnam's Sons, 1975. 158 p. B/w photos.

Stambler chronicles the record runs from the French Electric which went 39 mph in 1899 to the modern-day Blue Flame which set a record speed of 622 mph. Drivers covered include Malcolm and Donald Campbell, Art Arfons, Craig Breedlove, and Gary Gabelich. This is a run-of-the-mill account.

Tuthill, William R. SPEED ON SAND. Daytona Beach, Fla.: By the author, 1969. 50 p. Illus.

Tuthill tells the story of early speed runs on the sand at Daytona Beach, Florida. Tuthill begins his story with the 1902 attempts. Oval track stock car races, and cycle races are covered as well as the land speed record attempts. It was published by the author.

Villa, Leo, and Gray, Tony. THE RECORD BREAKERS: SIR MALCOLM AND DONALD CAMPBELL, LAND AND WATER SPEED KINGS OF THE 20TH CENTURY. London: Hamlyn, 1969. 160 p.

This saga of Malcolm and Donald Campbell, their "Bluebird" cars and boats, and their life-long pursuit of speed records has been written by a man who worked for them for most of those years. It is an excellent account of behind-the-scenes work for a record attempt.

Chapter 5

ANNUALS

AMERICAN RACING DRIVERS CLUB YEARBOOK. Langhorne, Pa. Photos.

The racing activities of the American Racing Drivers Club for the previous year are covered. The American Racing Drivers Club is the nation's oldest and largest midget auto racing organization having started in 1939. Short race reports and pictures are provided. Business office: 1448 Hollywood Ave., Langhorne, Pa. 19047.

AMSA YEARBOOK. Flemington, N.J.: American Mini Stock Association.

This details the previous season's activities in picture and story form. Tracks covered include Flemington Speedway, Nazareth Raceway, Grandview Speedway, Dorney Park, and the Pocono minichampionship. Business office: Roundabout Racing Enterprises, Box 554, Flemington, N.J. 08822.

AUTOCOURSE. Richmond, Surrey, Engl.: Hazleton Securities.

A fine addition to motorsport literature, AUTOCOURSE provides thorough and spectacular Grand Prix coverage. Each race is presented in detail including a complete feature writeup plus statistical data such as entries and practice times, starting grid, past race winners, results and retirements, fastest laps, a diagram of the circuit, points, and a lap chart. Added information includes results from the USA, Formula II, Formula III, Formula 5000, and Le Mans. Feature articles are also presented--biographical and historical. Business office: 1 Church Terrace, Richmond, Surrey, Engl., TW10 65E.

AUTOMOBILE ALMANAC. Nyack, N.Y.: Automobile Almanac. Index.

This is a round-up of the previous year's world and U.S. competitions. Famous race circuits, land speed records, motor racing history, word and picture glossaries are given. It covers FIA, AHRA, IMCA, NASCAR, NHRA, SCCA, and USAC and driver biographies. Some material on conventional street cars is provided. It is an excellent reference source. Business office: P.O. Box 32, Nyack, N.Y. 10960.

AUTOMOBILE YEAR. Newfoundland, N.J.: Haessner, No. 1--1953-54-- .

It is handsomely printed and includes marvelous photographs. Detailed and authoritative resumes of the year's international Grand Prix and sports car races are given. Each race report includes starting grid, fastest laps, retirements, and so forth. There is a report on the World Championship for rallies and articles on American and European championships. Feature articles--technical and biographical--are included, along with some general material on the automotive world at large. The first volume was published under the title ANNUAL AUTOMOBILE REVIEW. Business Office: P.O. Box 89, Newfoundland, N.J. 07435.

CAN-AM MIDGETS YEARBOOK. Kenmore, N.Y.: Can-Am Midgets Racing Club.

This work is comprised of pictures, stories, and reports of the racing season. Business office: P.O. Box 34, Kenmore, N.Y. 14217.

CHRIS SCHENKEL'S SPORTSCENE AUTO RACING. Vol. 1-1972. Dallas, Tex.: American Equity Press, 1972-74. Paperbound. Glossary.

This existed for at least two years before it ceased publication. It had several good feature stories that ranged from road racing and dragging to Indy cars and NASCAR. Business office: 1218 S. Ervay, Dallas, Tex. 75215.

CRA SPRINTER YEARBOOK. Huntington Beach: California Racing Association, 1968-69-- . Photos.

This yearbook varies as to frequency of publication. Some issues cover only one year while other issues span two years of competition. There are many good action photographs as well as numerous charts and tables. Business office: 10391 Maikai Drive, Huntington Beach, Calif. 92646.

DIRT TRACK'N "TEXAS" STYLE. Mesquite, Tex.: P and M Auto Racing Productions, 1976-- . Photos.

This annual covers drivers and races at the Devils Bowl race track near Dallas. In the future there are plans to include racing from other Texas tracks. It is very well done. Business Office: 1101 Birchwood Dr., Mesquite, Tex. 75149.

DOIN' IT IN THE DIRT. Natrona Hcts., Pa.: Triple-S-Publications. B/w photos.

This yearbook covers the western Pennsylvania dirt tracks. Business office: Box 373, Natrona Hcts., Pa. 15065.

DRAG RACING YEARBOOK. Los Angeles: Argus Publishers Corp. Photos.

POPULAR HOT RODDING'S yearbook provides complete coverage of NHRA, AHRA, and IHRA events of the previous year. Magazine format is utilized. Business Office: 12301 Wilshire Blvd., Los Angeles, Calif. 90025.

ENGINE ANNUAL. Los Angeles: Argus Publishers Corp. Illus.

In magazine format, this is a publication from POPULAR HOT RODDING. The 1978 issue featured many technical articles including material on Chevies, Fords, Vegas, Chryslers, Oldsmobiles, and Pontiacs. Pieces on blocks, rods, blower setups, and cams are included. Business office: 12301 Wilshire Blvd., Los Angeles, Calif. 90025.

FIA YEARBOOK OF AUTOMOBILE SPORT. Cambridge, Engl.: Patrick Stephens. Illus.

This is published under the authority of the Federation Internationale de l'Automobile and gives the current International Sporting Code. It has photographs and biographies of FIA graded drivers, pictures, and technical details of the world's leading competition cars, diagrams of circuits, a directory section, and schedule of events. Written in both English and French, it is a valuable reference work. Business Office: Haessner Publishing, P.O. Box 89, Newfoundland, N.J. 07435. (U.S. distributor.)

GATER RACING NEWS AUTO RACING YEARBOOK. Syracuse, N.Y.: Sports Trek. B/w photos.

Coverage includes racing activity in the entire Northeast from Canada to Florida. There are pictorial articles on limited sportsman, late models, super modifieds, sprint cars, asphalt and dirt modifieds, and late-model sportsman. Several biographical articles are also included. Business Office: P.O. Box 122, Syracuse, N.Y. 13201.

GRAND PRIX I-1960. Edited by Louis Stanley. New York: David McKay Co., 1960-- . Photos.

This annual is one of the best, discussing each event and the happenings that made it interesting. It is illustrated with photographs primarily of people rather than cars. Many of these are people rarely photographed--pit workers, mechanics, officials, managers, journalists, and the people behind the scene. It provides results and a list of champions but statistics are left to other annuals. Business office: David McKay Co., 750 Third Ave., New York, N.Y. 10017.

GRANDVIEW SPEEDWAY YEARBOOK. Langhorne, Pa. Photos.

This covers racing at the Grandview Speedway which is located in Bechtelsville, Pa. The yearbook provides short summaries of the races throughout the year. Business office: 1448 Hollywood Ave., Langhorne, Pa. 19047.

HOT ROD YEARBOOK. Los Angeles, Calif.: Petersen Publishing Co., 1962-- .

This annual covers drag racing, street rods, and technical articles. Business office: 8490 Sunset Blvd., Los Angeles, Calif. 90069.

IMCA YEARBOOK. Vinton, Iowa.: International Motor Contest Association, 1957?-- . Irregular.

The association racing season is covered. It started as early as 1957, perhaps earlier. They are now completing a combination 1975, 1976, 1977 racing season yearbook. Business office: P.O. Box 800, 421 First Ave., Vinton, Iowa 52349.

IMSA YEARBOOK. Fairfield, Conn.: International Motor Sports Association, 1972-- .

This provides excellent coverage of the previous year's racing of the International Motor Sports Association race by race. For each race the driver, car, laps, finishing and starting positions, and prize money is listed. Also listed are race length, time, fastest lap, and margin of victory. Separate tables include IMSA lap record holders, drivers, and points for the driver's championship. This annual is chock full of information. Business office: P.O. Box 805, Fairfield, Conn. 06430.

INDIANAPOLIS 500 MILE RACE ANNUAL. Speedway, Ind.: Central Publishing Co., 1974-75. Photos.

Donald Davidson's day-by-day coverage of action in May, features in-depth material on famous drivers, Davidson-type statistical box scores and biographical sketches of the participating drivers. The fan will enjoy the bonus coverage of the Ontario and Pocono 500s.

THE INDIANAPOLIS 500 YEARBOOK. Speedway, Ind.: Carl Hugness Publishing, 1973-- . Col. photos.

Complete coverage of the prestigious Indianapolis 500 mile race in diary format takes the reader through the month of May day-by-day. There is a detailed report of all race pit stops, plus feature articles, color photos of all starters with their cars and crews, and numerous race statistics and biographies. This is a treasury of information. Business office: Box 24308, Speedway, Ind. 46224.

INTERNATIONAL MOTOR RACING. Edited by Barrie Gill. New York: Two Continents, 1977-- . Photos.

Mainly Grand Prix but this covers the season in detail including grids, full team personnel and addresses. Some U.S. road racing and SCCA races are sketchily covered. It is a book format. Business office: 30 E. Forty-second St., New York, N.Y. 10017.

JOHN PLAYER MOTORSPORT YEARBOOK. New York: Collier Books. Illus.

Extensive coverage of the racing season in Formula I, Sports Cars, Formula II, Formula 5000, Formula Atlantic, and Formula Ford, and the World Rallying Championship, and British Rallying is provided. For Formula I the starting grid, results, and retirements are listed for each race. Short biographies of the most distinguished drivers are provided. It is well done! Business office: 866 Third Ave., New York, N.Y. 10022.

KARS DIRT CIRCUIT. Mechanicsburg, Pa.

This annual covers the tracks of Hagerstown, Williams Grove, and Selinsgrove in Pennsylvania with stories, race results, and photos. Business office: 1 Speedway Dr., Mechanicsburg, Pa. 17055.

MAINE RACING ANNUAL. Falmouth, Maine: 1975-- . Photos.

This photo history of the oval track season in Maine has very little text but is nicely done. Business office: 547 Blackstrap Rd., Falmouth, Maine 04105.

MIDWEST SPEEDWAYS YEARBOOK. Milwaukee, Wis.: 1975-- .

This yearbook covers late-model and sportsman stock car racing at the Hales Corners and Cedarburg Speedways in the Milwaukee area. It is published in June. Business office: 6646 West Fairview Ave., Milwaukee, Wis. 53213.

MOTORCOURSE. Vol. 1--1976-77. New York: Arco Publishing Co., 1976-77-- . Hardbound. Illus.

This gives a race-by-race account of the year's Grand Prix season with full statistics on practice times, race times, championship points, and race results. A diagram of each circuit is provided. It covers other major motorcycle racing services and has personality features on top riders. Business office: 219 Park Ave., South, New York, N.Y. 10003.

MOTOR CYCLE NEWS YEARBOOK. Newfoundland, N.J.: Haessner.

This annual is prepared by writers of MOTOR CYCLE NEWS. Statistical data from the season plus material on speedway, motocross, grass track, ice racing, hillclimbs, and sand track are included. All world and national championships are covered. Business office: P.O. Box 89, Newfoundland, N.J. 07435.

MOTORCYCLE YEAR. Lausanne, Switzerland: Edita S.A., 1975-76-- . Photos.

This is a handsome bound volume that combines information on the motorcycle industry with results of the competition year. There is good coverage of motocross. Action photos and complete tables of results are elaborate and complete. Business office: 3 rue de la Vigie, 1000 Lausanne 9, Switzerland.

THE MOTOR RACING YEAR. New York: W.W. Norton, 1969-- . Hardbound. Photos.

This is a comprehensive review of the year's international motor racing. It provides a full report of all the events in the Formula I Championship of Drivers and the Sports Car Manufacturers' Championship. In addition, there are accounts of the Formula II championship, the European 2-liter Constructors' Championship for Sports Cars, the Can-Am Series, and Indianapolis and Tasman racing results. Business office: 500 Fifth Ave., New York, N.Y. 10036.

NARC YEARBOOK. Calistoga, Calif.: Northern Auto Racing Club, 1969-- . Photos.

NARC is a sprint car organization. The annual is primarily photographic coverage of the club's past season. Photos and biographies of the top ten finishers plus name and photo of all other participants (over one hundred) are published. Short summaries of all races plus a run-down of finishers are supplied. Business office: 1002 Manor Blvd., San Leandro, Calif. 94579.

NCRA YEARBOOK. Yukon, Okla.: National Championship Racing Association, 1972-- .

The NCRA Yearbook is a yearly roundup of race results and driver profiles from the National Championship Racing Association. It covers competition in the Southwest. Business office: 11525 Carriage Dr., Yukon, Okla. 73099.

THE OUTLAW ANNUAL. Speedway, Ind.: Carl Hungness Publishing, 1978-- . Illus.

This illustrated annual covers all parts of the United States. Business office: Carl Hungness Publishing, P.O. Box 24308-D, Speedway, Ind. 46224.

POSTSCRIPT TO POCONO. Kokomo, Ind.: Tim-Mel Publications, 1971-- . Photos.

The 1971 issue is the only one published to date. This is pictorial coverage by Glen Banner of the inaugural 500 mile race for Indy cars at Pocono International Raceway in Pennsylvania. Race statistics are included for each competing car and driver. The photography and layout are excellent. Business office: 1609 S. LaFountain, Kokomo, Ind. 46901.

PUROLATOR MEDIA GUIDE. Rahway, N.J.: Purolator, 1974-- . Diags.

Published by Purolator and distributed to the media to help them cover NASCAR Grand National racing, "Pit Notes" are included for each track to aid the writer in developing a story line. A diagram of each track is included. Information on the Purolator-sponsored car and driver is emphasized. Business office: Purolator Filter Division, Purolator, Inc., Rahway, N.J. 07065.

RACING ANNUAL. New York: Car and Driver, 1967-1970.

It rounds up articles on international road racing, U.S. road racing, the USAC championship circuit, stock car racing, the Indianapolis 500, Le Mans, Daytona, Canadian-American Challenge Cup, Trans-American Sedan Series, and the American Road Race of Champions. A list of the 100 top drivers from the previous year is included. Business office: One Park Ave., New York, N.Y. 10010.

RACING CAR YEAR. Newport Beach, Calif.: Bond/Parkhurst Publications, 1973.

This annual has been published only once so far--1973. It is a book by Jonathan Thompson covering the race cars that compete in Formula I, Formula II, Formula 5000, USAC, Can-Am Interseries, 3-Liter, 2-Liter, Special Grand Touring, and Special Touring events. For each make the author has listed the manufacturer, entrant, drivers, major sponsors, colors, types, engine, gearbox, suspension, brakes, wheels, tires, chassis, fuel capacity, dimensions, and weight. It is a valuable illustrated and indexed gold mine of information. Business office: Drawer B, Newfoundland, N.J. 07435.

RACING SCENE INDIANAPOLIS 500. Indianapolis: Motor Publications, 1971. Discontinued. Photos.

This particular annual was published one year only. It is an excellent compilation of text and photos on the famous Indianapolis 500. There is daily coverage of prerace practice and qualifications plus technical data, pit stops, and track records. They have compiled a complete race story, including the victory banquet.

SPRINT CAR PICTORIAL. Indianapolis: Crucean/Mahoney Adventures, 1969-- . Photos.

This is excellent year-end coverage of the USAC sprint circuit with photographic coverage of each race plus reportorial comment. Flip sequences and human interest shots add to this yearbook's value. It also carries similiar coverage of the USAC dirt champ series. Business office: 2710 Cold Stream Ln., 1-B, Indianapolis, Ind. 46220.

STREET MACHINES AND BRACKET RACING. Los Angeles: Petersen Publishing Co., 1978-- . Photos.

Bracket racing is gaining rapidly in popularity and this new Petersen publication will greatly contribute to that growth. Bracket racing is handicap competition for the nonprofessional sportsman--scale drag racer, with handicaps determined by the contestants themselves. Articles on the cars, drivers, and technical data are provided. Business office: 8490 Sunset Blvd., Los Angeles, Calif. 90069.

USAC MIDGET ANNUAL. Speedway, Ind.: Carl Hungness Publishing, 1978-- .

This annual covers midget competition of the United States Auto Club. It is illustrated. Business office: Carl Hungness Publishing, P.O. Box 24308-D, Speedway, Ind. 46224.

USAC YEARBOOK. Speedway, Ind.: 1956-- .

The USAC YEARBOOK is essentially a statistical wrap-up of the season. It contains lists of USAC officers, officials, committees, and life members. A complete summary of race results for each division is given along with a listing of all USAC sanctioned tracks and their locations. A USAC active driver registry is also included. It is illustrated with photographs. Business office: 4910 W. Sixteenth St., Speedway, Ind. 46224.

Chapter 6

PERIODICALS

For purposes of this chapter we have listed under newsletters various minor racing publications, club notes, or business releases regardless of format. Under magazines we have listed all major racing publications including many in tabloid form.

A. MAGAZINES

AMA NEWS. Westerville, Ohio: American Motorcyclist Association, 1947-- . Monthly.

This covers all aspects of motorcycling including professional and amateur competition, touring, technical features, interviews, profiles, legislation, and history. Business office: Box 141, Westerville, Ohio 43081.

AREA AUTO RACING NEWS. Trenton, N.J.: Leonard Sammons, Jr., 1963-- . 50 issues yearly.

This newspaper format covers racing on all levels in the northeastern United States especially in New York, New Jersey, Pennsylvania, and Connecticut. Numerous race reports from small tracks are furnished. Business office: 2829 S. Broad St., Trenton, N.J. 08610.

AUTO RACING DIGEST. Evanston, Ill.: Century Publishing Co., 1973-- . Bimonthly.

This carries articles on all phases of racing with particular emphasis on USAC and NASCAR races and drivers. It is not a race report paper but a magazine with fairly in-depth articles. There are many driver profiles. Business office: 1020 Church St., Evanston, Ill. 60201.

AUTO RACING MONTHLY MAGAZINE. Trenton, N.J.: Leonard Sammons,

Jr., 1975-- . 10 issues yearly.

This appears in a magazine format but it is not a polished effort. The publication leans to driver profiles and small think pieces rather than race results. It profiles area drivers, but includes at least two major drivers per issue. Business office: 2829 S. Broad St., Trenton, N.J. 08610.

AUTOSPORT. London: Haymarket Publishing, 1950-- . Weekly.

Published every Thursday, AUTOSPORT is one of the oldest and most respected offerings of the motoring press. Its outlook is primarily British, but major international events are covered in some detail. Grand Prix coverage is excellent. Local coverage of events throughout Britain is also very good. Business office: Regent House, 54-62 Regent St., London, Engl.

AUTOSPORT CANADA. Mississauga, Ont.: Wheelspin News, 1974-- . Monthly.

A magazine devoted to automobile sport and the events and activities of the Canadian Automobile Sports Club, AUTOSPORT CANADA emphasizes road racing and rallying. A special feature is ice racing schedules. Business office: 3057 Universal Dr., Mississauga, Ont. L4X 2E2.

AUTO SPORTS WEEKLY. Arlington, Va.: Mike Maiatico, Weekly.

Business office: 3806 S. Four Mile Run Dr., Arlington, Va. 22206.

AUTOWEEK. Formerly COMPETITION PRESS, COMPETITION PRESS AND AUTOWEEK and AUTOWEEK AND COMPETITION PRESS. Reno, Nev.: Real Resources Group, 1958-- . Weekly.

This newspaper format deals with all automotive topics, concentrating on competition. It covers industry in the United States and abroad and offers some coverage of off-road and recreational vehicles. Business office: Box A, Reno, Nev. 89506.

BIG BIKE. Encino, Calif.: Hi-Torque Publications, 1968-- . Monthly.

This concerns itself with motorcycle drag racing and motorcycle road racing and is distributed worldwide with emphasis on North America and Europe. Business office: 16200 Ventura Blvd., Suite 213, Encino, Calif. 91316.

CAR AND DRIVER. New York: 1957-- . Monthly.

This is a general interest automotive magazine with space devoted to auto racing--actual competition plus features both past and present on personalities in competition. Business office: One Park Ave., New York, N.Y. 10016.

CAR CRAFT. Los Angeles, Calif.: 1953-- . Monthly.

This is a general automotive magazine with drag racing articles, technical features, "how-to" articles, and general automotive pieces. Interviews, profiles, and photos are also present. Business office: 8490 Sunset Blvd., Los Angeles, Calif. 90069.

CARS MAGAZINE. New York: Popular Publications, 1957-- . Monthly.

The main emphasis is on hot rods and drag racing. Published in magazine format their racing features include personality profiles, race coverage of big drag events, and race car building. The material varies with each issue. Some historical and nostalgic material emerges. Business office: 420 Lexington Ave., Suite 2540, New York, N.Y. 10017.

CAVALCADE OF AUTO RACING. Worcester, Mass.: Cavalcade Publications, 1978-- . 40 issues yearly.

This tabloid format features short racing reports from around the United States covering all types of competition racing. There are many lengthy regular columns that present more details about racing personnel, both past and present, than are usually found in papers of this type. There is some feature material. Business office: P.O. Box 367, Worcester, Mass. 01613.

CHECKERED FLAG RACING NEWS. Watertown, Wis.: John A. Quinn, 31 issues yearly.

Business office: P.O. Box 314, 118 W. Main St., Watertown, Wis. 53094.

CHECKERED FLAG STOCK CAR. Richmond, Va.: Bob Johnson. 18 issues yearly.

Business office: Racing Newspaper, Inc., P.O. Box 13046, Richmond, Va. 23225.

CYCLE ILLUSTRATED. New York: National Newstand Publications, 1978-- . Bimonthly.

This covers all aspects of motorcycling including technical bike pieces and competition news. It has a new products section and regular columns. Business office: 257 Park Ave., South, New York, N.Y. 10010.

CYCLE NEWS EAST. Tucker, Ga.: 1968-- . Weekly.

This publication covers motorcycle races and events of all kinds with emphasis on inside views of competition. Personality profiles, reports on legislative developments and machine tests round out the package. The dividing line between CYCLE NEWS WEST's area of coverage and CYCLE NEWS EAST's area of coverage is the Mississippi River. CYCLE NEWS DIXIE, which first appeared in January 1970, merged with CYCLE NEWS EAST in 1972 to form the present CYCLE NEWS EAST. Business office: Box 805, Tucker, Ga. 30084.

CYCLE NEWS WEST. Long Beach, Calif.: 1965-- . Weekly.

This western version covers motorcycle races and events of all kinds with emphasis on inside views of competition. Personality profiles, reports on legislative developments, and machine tests round out the package. The dividing line between CYCLE NEWS WEST's area of coverage and CYCLE NEWS EAST's area of coverage is the Mississippi River. Business Office: P.O. Box 498, Long Beach, Calif. 90801.

CYCLE TIMES. Chicago: Multi-Media Publications, 1975-- . Monthly.

This is a midwestern cycle publication in tabloid format. There is general motorcycle news as well as race coverage and interviews. Business office: 222 W. Adams St., Suite 895, Chicago, Ill. 60606.

CYCLE WORLD. Newport Beach, Calif.: Bond/Parkhurst, 1962-- . Monthly.

This magazine format includes features on special bikes, road tests, racers, and racing events, and technical features. There is a regular competition report column "Race Watch." Business office: 1499 Monrovia Ave., Newport Beach, Calif. 92663.

DIRT BIKE. Encino, Calif.: Hi-Torque Publications, 1971-- . Monthly.

The scope here is all forms of off-road motorcycle riding including racing. The magazine has no geographical limitations and is heavily distributed in Europe. Business office: 16200 Ventura Blvd., Suite 213, Encino, Calif. 91316.

DIRT RIDER. Canoga Park, Calif.: Monthly.

This is concerned with field competition. Business address: 7950 Deering Ave., Canoga Park, Calif. 91304.

DRAG REVIEW MAGAZINE. Bristol, Tenn.: International Hot Rod Association, 1971-- . Monthly.

Drag racing coverage with heavy emphasis on IHRA events is the aim of this publication. Black-and-white photos meet results and records, and some driver profiles are included. Business office: P.O. Box 3029, Bristol, Tenn. 37620.

DUNE BUGGIES AND HOT VW'S. Costa Mesa, Calif.: Wright Publishing Co., 1967-- . Monthly.

"How-to's" as well as technical and competition articles are included in this magazine format. Business office: P.O. Box 2260, Costa Mesa, Calif. 92626.

FLORIDA STOCK CAR NEWS. Winter Haven, Fla.: Roland Palot, 8 issues yearly.

This publication is sold at race tracks only. Business office: P.O. Box 2194 Winter Haven, Fla. 33880.

FORMULA. Santa Ana, Calif.: Formula Enterprises, 1974-- . Monthly.

Known as America's international auto racing magazine, this periodical is actually devoted primarily to sports car racing--Formula I, Grand Prix, professional road racing in America, and important SCCA national races. Profiles and interviews plus race car tests, help make this an excellent publication. Business office: 2020 S. Susan, Suite L, Santa Ana, Calif. 92704.

GATER RACING NEWS. Syracuse, N.Y.: Sports Trek, 1965-- . 33 issues yearly.

It covers oval racing of all types including the entire east from Canada to Florida. It also covers major racing events all over the United States and the world. It is published weekly from May through October and once a month from November through April. Business office: P.O. Box 122, Syracuse, N.Y. 13201.

GOODYEAR MOTOR SPORTS CLUB CHALLENGE. Akron, Ohio: Goodyear Tire and Rubber Co., 1975-1976. Quarterly.

This magazine ceased publication at the end of 1976 when the Motor Sports Club ceased operation. It was a well-done magazine that carried several feature articles per issue on all phases of racing--USAC championship, rallying, SCCA, NASCAR, drag racing, and formula cars. There were good biographical pieces, and it was illustrated--color and black-and-white. Business office: 1144 E. Market St., Akron, Ohio 44316.

GRAND NATIONAL SCENE. Notasulga, Ala.: Robert E. Griggs, Jr., 25 issues yearly.

Business office: P.O. Box 309. Notasulga, Ala. 36866.

HAWKEYE RACING NEWS. Vinton, Iowa: Keith Knaack, 1967-- . Irregular.

This tabloid format covers all types of racing throughout the midwestern states. It prints weekly April through September and publishes three or four special editions throughout the winter months. Business office: Box 800, Vinton, Iowa 52349.

HOT BIKE. Anaheim, Calif.: TRM Publications, 1977-- . Monthly.

Cycle magazine containing road tests, technical pieces, race reports, and feature articles. A "Hot Bike Calendar" section lists race dates. Business office: 2145 W. LaPalma, Anaheim, Calif. 92801.

HOT ROD. Los Angeles: 1948-- . Monthly.

This magazine format covers drag racing and street machines. Technical articles, "how-to's", interviews, profiles, and new product news are a part of this standard in the field. Business office: 8490 Sunset Blvd., Los Angeles, Calif. 90069.

ILLUSTRATED SPEEDWAY NEWS. Massapequa, N.Y.: Walter E. Bull, 1937-- . Weekly.

Columns, race reports, schedules, articles, and photographs are included in this newspaper format. Business office: 83 Grand Ave., Massapequa, N.Y. 11758.

KARTER NEWS. Covina, Calif.: International Kart Federation. Monthly.

This magazine format covers the racing activities of the International Kart Federation. Regular departments cover club news and schedules. It is illustrated. Business office: 416 S. Grand, Covina, Calif. 91724.

KARTING. Edited by A.T. Burgess. Chislehurst, Engl.: Karting Magazine, 1960-- . Monthly.

Business office: Bank House, Summerhills, Chislehurst, Kent, Engl.

KARTING DIGEST. Miami: K-Dee Publishing Co., 1974-- . Monthly.

Business office: 1997 N.E. 150th St., Miami, Fla. 33181.

MID-AMERICAN AUTO RACING NEWS. Toledo: Mid-American Publishing

Co., 1971-- . Irregular.

This publication covers short track oval racing competition in a seven-state area: Ohio, Michigan, Kentucky, West Virginia, Indiana, eastern Illinois, and western Pennsylvania. MAARN is published weekly from mid-April through mid-October but monthly otherwise. Business office: 10430 Airport Hwy., Box 226, Swanton, Ohio 43558.

MIDWEST RACER. Urbana, Ill.: 1977-- . Irregular.

A new entry in the Midwest collection of racing tabloids, this publication covers both local short track racing and major U.S. races. It has a clean sharp look in both print and photographs. It is published monthly January, February, March, November, and December and weekly April through October. Business office: Urbana, Ill.

MIDWEST RACING NEWS. Milwaukee, Wis.: Midwest Racing News, 1959-- . 25 issues yearly.

This tabloid format covers short track stock, modified, sprint, and midget racing in the Midwest, plus major USAC and NASCAR events throughout the United States. It is published weekly May through September and monthly in April, October, and December. (It was published under the title MIDWEST RACING NEWS until (1978.) Business office: 6646 W. Fairview Ave., Milwaukee, Wis. 53213.

MODERN CYCLE. Canoga Park, Calif.: Challenge Publications. Monthly.

This is a general approach to motorcycling with technical and feature articles as well as some competition pieces. There are regular columns. Merged with DIRT RIDER and STREET BIKE. Business office: 7950 Deering Ave., Canoga Park, Calif. 91304.

MODERN MOTOR. Sydney, Australia: 1954-- . Monthly.

This concentrates on Formula I with a preview story before the season and coverage of each Grand Prix with photos. It also covers events such as the London to Sydney marathon. It does not cover Australian motorsport with the exception of the yearly production touring car race at the Mt. Panorma circuit at Bathurst N.S.W. Business office: 15 Boundary St., 3rd Floor, Rushcutters Bay, Sydney, N.S.W., Australia 2011.

MOTOCROSS ACTION. Encino, Calif.: Hi-Torque Publications, 1973-- . Monthly.

It is specifically concerned with and limited to motocross racing, a form of off-road, closed-track, natural terrain motorcycle racing which is popular in the United States and Europe. Business office: 16200 Ventura Blvd., Suite 213, Encino, Calif. 91316.

MOTORCYCLE WEEKLY. Paramount, Calif.: Press Work Publishers, 1969-- . Weekly.

This newspaper format covers news in the world of cycling and has detailed reports on motorcycle track events. Business office: 15470 Paramount Blvd., Paramount, Calif. 90723.

MOTORCYCLE WORLD. New York: Countrywide Publications. Bimonthly.

This is a general cycle publication but devotes space each month to competition events. Also it has a regular column titled "Riders to Racers," road tests, features, and technical pieces. Business office: 257 Park Ave., South, New York, N.Y. 10010.

MOTOR CYCLIST. Sierra Madre, Calif.: Petersen Publishing Co., 1912-- . Monthly.

It covers all aspects of cycling including competition. Business office: 8490 Sunset Blvd., Los Angeles, Calif. 90069.

MOTOR SPORT BULLETIN. Paris, France: Federation International de l'Automobile. Monthly.

This publication carries material in both French and English. It lists sporting regulations, technical information, results of FIA sanctioned events, dates of international racing events, and an extremely valuable section giving the addresses of racing organizers all over the world. U.S. business address: Automobile Competition Committee for the United States, FIA, Inc., Suite 302, 1725 K St. NW, Washington, D.C. 20006.

MOTORACING NEWS. Orange, Calif.: Mobius Press, 1978. Weekly.

This is a new tabloid format racing paper that competes favorably with those papers already on the market. The layout is appealing, the coverage widespread, and the writing interesting. Business office: 852 N. Main St., Orange, Calif. 92668.

MOTORSPORTS PICTORIAL. Hamburg, N.Y.: Carl Fredricksen. 8 issues yearly.

Business office: P.O. Box 353, Hamburg, N.Y. 14075.

MOTORSPORTS WEEKLY. Newport Beach, Calif.: Action Publishers, 1976-- . Weekly.

This newspaper format covers all types of U.S. racing including motorcycle racing. Many brief news articles and race reports are interspersed with regular columns as well as a few longer feature stories. There are many photographs and some technical pieces. Business office: P.O. Box 2880, Newport Beach, Calif. 99263.

MOTOR TREND. Los Angeles: 1949-- . Monthly.

This is a general automotive magazine that covers motorsport competitions as a part of its national appeal. Money-saving ideas for the motorist, high performance features, interviews, and at least one competition-related articles, interview, or race report are usual per issue. Business office: 8490 Sunset Blvd., Los Angeles, Calif. 90069.

NATIONAL DRAGSTER. North Hollywood, Calif.: National Hot Rod Association, 1960-- . Weekly for 50 weeks yearly.

The editorial coverage in this tabloid is given to the latest drag racing news, including weekly performance reports, in-depth coverage of NHRA national and world championship events. Personality profiles, special interest features, rule updates, and technical and new product information are included. Business office: P.O. Box 150, North Hollywood, Calif. 91603.

NATIONAL SPEED SPORT NEWS. Formerly NATIONAL AUTO RACING NEWS. Ridgewood, N.J.: Kay Publishing Co., 1932-- . 50 issues yearly.

NSSN is the premier tabloid covering auto racing including short track and major events throughout the United States. It also covers major racing outside the United States. There are occasional feature articles and regular columns. NSSN began using their present title during war years 1941-1945. It first appeared as the NATIONAL AUTO RACING NEWS, supplement to the BERGEN HERALD. Then it changed to its present tabloid format in 1934. Business office: News Building, P.O. Box 608, Ridgewood, N.J. 07451.

NEW ENGLAND SPEEDWAY SCENE. North Easton, Mass.: Val Le Sieur. Weekly.

Business address: P.O. Box 300, North Easton, Mass. 02356.

OFF-ROAD. Los Angeles: Argus Publishers Corp. Monthly.

Combined with OFF-VEHICLES and OFF-ROAD VEHICLES AND ADVENTURE, this general publication is devoted to all aspects of off-road vehicle enjoyment. It covers off-road competition events like the Baja 1000 kilometers. Many technical articles are included. Business office: 12301 Wilshire Blvd., Los Angeles, Calif. 90025.

OFF ROAD ACTION NEWS. Westminster, Calif. Monthly.

This is a tabloid format devoted to off-road racing which has long feature articles on competition. There are regular columns and excellent coverage of the sport. Business office: 9371 Kramer, Suite C, Westminister, Calif. 92683.

OFF-ROAD ADVERTISER. Lakewood, Calif. Monthly.

It features coverage of all major off-road races but the publication is primarily known for a large classified ad section on competition vehicles and many pages of ads on high performance parts. Business office: P.O. Box 340, Lakewood, Calif. 90714.

O.R.V. Canoga Park, Calif.: Challenge Publications. Monthly.

O.R.V. is a magazine of off-roading with mostly technical and nonracing coverage but one feature a month is normally geared to a competitive event. Business office: 7950 Deering Ave., Canoga Park, Calif. 91304.

POPULAR HOT RODDING. Los Angeles: Argus Publishers Corp. Monthly.

This is a general hot rod publication covering technical and feature articles on both street and strip rods. It has several regular columns and more technical articles than others of this type. It is well done. Business office: 12301 Wilshire Blvd., Los Angeles, Calif. 90025.

PROSPEED REVUE. Brockton, Mass.: Phil Harris. 17 issues yearly.

Business office: P.O. Box 1463, Brockton, Mass. 02403.

RACEWORLD PHOTO MONTHLY. Syracuse, N.Y.: Nan-Way Publications, 1975-- . Monthly.

A tabloid publication offering photographic coverage of auto racing in the northeastern United States, this offers very little written material but there is large-size, well-done photography--driver sequences, photo essays of major races, and flip sequences from the present and the past. Business office: Box 65, Salina Station, Syracuse, N.Y. 13208.

RACEWORLD RACING REVIEW. Syracuse, N.Y.: Nan-Way Publications, 1974-- . Irregular.

A tabloid publication with good photographs, this tends to cover racing in the northeastern United States. It has race reports, feature stories, columns, and driver profiles. Business office: Box 65, Salina Station, Syracuse, N.Y. 13208.

RACING CAR NEWS. New South Wales, Australia, 1961-- . Monthly.

This is an Australian motor racing publication that covers Australian motorsports events, primarily championship races, but there is also some international coverage. Business office: 177 Lawson St., Redfern, N.S.W., Australia 2016.

RACING CARS. Speedway, Ind.: Carl Hungness and Associates, 1977-- . Quarterly.

This new publication covers only American oval track racing, including sprints, championship cars, midgets, and stock cars. Stories on racing personalities, race tracks, nostalgia articles as well as human and in-depth interviews are found in most issues. Color and black-and-white photographs are excellent and plentiful. Most articles are feature stories. It is one of very few magazines devoted exclusively to oval track racing. Business office: Box 24308-K, Speedway, Ind. 46224.

RACING PICTORIAL MAGAZINE. Indianapolis: Ray Mann, 1959-- . Quarterly.

This is pictorial coverage of auto racing in America covering the events which occur in the three months featured in a given issue. Most issues have a special color section up to sixteen pages showing top drivers and/or their cars. It covers USAC, NASCAR, SCCA, ARCA, and Formula 5000. Business office: P.O. Box 500B, Indianapolis, Ind. 46206.

RACING WHEELS. Vol. 17--1978. Vancouver, Wash.: 40 issues yearly.

This is a tabloid published weekly April through November and every other week during the off-season. It covers oval track auto racing of all types--stock cars, sprints, midgets, and modifieds (USAC, NASCAR, IMSA). Its unofficial motto is to "serve the grass roots of auto racing." Business office: P.O. Box 1535, Vancouver, Wash. 98663.

RALLYE MAGAZINE: Dallas, Tex.: 1975-1977(?). Monthly.

It covered road rally competition and published articles that include actual competition results, rally personalities, technical articles on rally cars, and new products. Articles could be used by average rally drivers. Business office: 2880 LBJ Freeway, Suite 243, Dallas, Tex. 75234.

RALLY NEWS. Arlington, Tex.: n.d. Monthly.

This new publication in the rally field is a newspaper format of interest to TSD and performance rallyists. Business office: 1720 Glynn Oaks, Arlington, Tex. 76010.

REVS MOTORCYCLE NEWS. New South Wales, Australia: Modern Magazines, 1967-- . Biweekly.

This is a general interest motorcycle magazine with reports of world championship meetings and other major overseas events, plus wide coverage of Australian motorcycle sports. Business office: Ryrie House, 15 Boundary St., Rushcutters Bay, New South Wales, Australia 2011.

ROAD AND TRACK. Newport Beach, Calif.: CBS Publications, 1947-- . Monthly.

For knowledgeable car enthusiasts, this magazine carries car tests, driver profiles, and general automotive articles. It usually carries two or three competition reports each month--Grand Prix or major USAC races receive priority treatment. Business office: 1499 Monrovia Ave., Newport Beach, Calif. 92663.

ROAD RACERS MAGAZINE. Clearwater, Fla.: Kirk Publishing Co., 1977-- . 10 issues yearly.

This periodical is devoted to nationwide coverage of amateur and semipro road racing. The initial issue contained among other materials an article on Dan Gurney's Formula Ford Eagles, coverage of the second annual Daytona classic and numerous race reports. There are color and black-and-white photos. Business address: P.O. Box 4532, Clearwater, Fla. 33518.

SCORE INTERNATIONAL NEWS. Canoga Park, Calif.: SCORE International, 1973-- . Bimonthly.

SCORE is devoted to off-road racing. Published in a tabloid format, it began as a quarterly. Sometimes it is listed under SCORE NEWS. The scope of the publication is international. It features action reports on SCORE races, racers, and anything pertinent to the sport of off-road racing. Business office: 20944 Sherman Way, Suite 115, Canoga Park, Calif. 91303.

SOUTHERN AUTO RACING NEWS. Notasulga, Ala.: Robert E. Graggs, Jr. Monthly.

Business office: P.O. Box 309, Notasulga, Ala. 36866.

SOUTHERN MOTORACING. Winston-Salem, N.C.: Universal Services, 1964-- . 25 issues yearly.

This publication, printed in a newspaper format, covers racing in the southern states extending also to the East Coast. There is major coverage of the larger races--NASCAR, SCCA, USAC but also reports from the smaller southern tracks, and some biographical material. Business office: 1049 Northwest Blvd., Winston-Salem, N.C. 27101.

SOUTHERN MOTORSPORTS JOURNAL. Opp, Ala.: Bob Hoffman. 40 issues yearly.

Business office: P.O. Drawer 637, Opp, Ala. 36467.

SOUTHWEST RACING NEWS. Garland, Tex.: Bill Gray. Monthly.

Business office: P.O. Box 4D333, Garland, Tex. 75040.

SPEED JOURNAL. Colorado Springs, Colo.: Adman Publishers. Monthly.

Business office: 320 E. Victoria, Colorado Springs, Colo. 80903.

SPORTS CAR. Santa Ana, Calif.: Paul Oxman Publishing, 1944-- . Monthly.

This magazine is the official publication of the Sports Car Club of America. It is sent to every regular member of SCCA and has a large complimentary list of other automotive and race related people. It contains feature articles, reports of SCCA events, and regular columns as well as updating regulations and schedules. It also publishes race and rally results. Business office: 3629 W. Warner Ave., Santa Ana, Calif. 92704.

STOCK CAR RACING MAGAZINE. Alexandria, Va.: Lopez Publications, 1966-- . Monthly.

This magazine contains articles on stock car drivers, cars, and races. Business office: 1420 Prince St., Alexandria, Va. 22314.

SUPER CHEVY MAGAZINE. Los Angeles, Calif.: Argus Publishers Corp., 1973-- . Bimonthly.

This magazine is for enthusiasts who build and race their own cars. Technical features, race reports, interviews, profiles, and new products information are included. Business office: 12301 Wilshire Blvd., Los Angeles, Calif. 90025.

SUPER STOCK AND DRAG ILLUSTRATED. Alexandria, Va.: Lopez Publications, 1964-- . Monthly.

Drag racing and high performance automobiles are covered. Road tests, technical articles, "how-to" columns, race reports, biographical sketches are included. Business office: 1420 Prince St., Alexandria, Va. 22314.

TRAVELIN' 4 X 4 'S AND OFF-ROAD VEHICLES. Sherman Oaks, Calif.: E-Go Enterprises. Monthly.

This publication, produced in magazine format, covers off-road vehicles including race reports and technical articles. Business office: P.O. Box 5755, Sherman Oaks, Calif. 91423.

TRI-STATE AUTO RACING NEWS. Greensburg, Pa.: Norwin Printing Co., 1968-- . Weekly from late April through mid-September.

This publication covers short tracks (third mile and half mile) in depth in western Pennsylvania, eastern Ohio, and West Virginia. It provides local drivers with publicity but does not cover national news. Business office: 567 N. Main St., Greensburg, Pa. 15601.

TRI-STATE SPEED PRESS. College Park, Md.: Dick Jones. 40 issues yearly.

Business office: 4814 Hollywood Rd., College Park, Md. 20740.

USAC MAGAZINE. Speedway, Ind.: United States Auto Club, 1970-75. Irregular.

This discontinued magazine carried articles about USAC drivers from all divisions, recaps of races, and featured new cars and developments in USAC. It was illustrated with photographs.

VOLKSWAGEN GREATS. Los Angeles: Coronado Book Corp. Bimonthly.

Devoted primarily to technical and noncompetitive articles on Volkswagens, this publication occasionally does have a piece on such competitive events as the Baja 1000. Business office: 12301 Wilshire Blvd., Los Angeles, Calif. 90025.

WESTERN RACING NEWS. Peoria, Ariz.: Pueble Publishers, vol. 7, 1978. Irregular. Photos.

This tabloid publication is published weekly March through October and then once a month November through February. It does a good job of covering racing in the western United States. The columns are informative and entertaining. Business office: P.O. Box 998, Peoria, Ariz. 85345.

WHEELSPIN NEWS. Formerly INTERNATIONAL WHEELSPIN NEWS. Mississauga, Ont.: Wheelspin News, 1965-- . Biweekly.

This publication deals primarily with Canadian motorsports of all types. It does cover major U.S. events in USAC, NASCAR, and SCCA competition. Race reports, columns, technical articles, and photographs are included in this newspaper format. Business address: 3057 Universal Dr., Mississauga, Ont. L4X 2E2.

B. NEWSLETTERS

AMERICAN AUTO RACING WRITERS AND BROADCASTERS ASSOCIATION NEWSLETTER. Burbank, Calif. Monthly.

The newsletter contains schedule of events for members. It reports on regional officers, on media relationships with different race tracks and on new publications of members. Business office: 922 N. Pass Ave., Burbank, Calif. 91505.

ARROW NEWSLETTER. Fairfield, Conn.: International Motor Sports Association. Irregular.

The newsletter is published whenever there is news to be communicated to members. Race results and racing schedules are included. Business office: P.O. Box 805, Fairfield, Conn. 06430.

CAMS REPORT. Victoria, Australia: Confederation of Australian Motor Sport. Irregular.

This is in a leaflet form and is an information guide four-to-six pages in length. It gives news of the organization, an occasional book review, rules and regulations, and calendar changes. Business office: 382 Burke Rd., Camberwell, Victoria, Australia.

CHEVY HOT LINE. Santa Ana, Calif.: Steve Smith Autosports, 1976-- . Monthly.

This publication gives information on high performance Chevrolets for race track, strip, and street. The major emphasis is on engines but includes material on other areas such as drivelines and rear-ends. Business office: P.O. Box 11631, Santa Ana, Calif. 92711.

CLUTCH CHATTER. Indianapolis: 1977-- . Monthly.

This newspaper format publication contains news of interest to the Indianapolis region of the Sports Car Club of America. Short features, schedule news, race reports, and rule changes are included. Business office: 940 N. Pennsylvania St., Indianapolis, Ind. 46204.

DATSUNEWS. Brea, Calif.: Datsun Owners Clubs Association. Quarterly.

This newsletter covers news of interest to Datsun owners including competition reports and some good rally information. Business office: Box 41, Brea, Calif. 92621.

FINISH LINE. Formerly CALIFORNIA SPORTS CAR and POST GRID. Hollywood, Calif.: 1948-- . Monthly.

This is presently a four-to-six page newsletter of the California Sports Car Club region of SCCA. It covers news of general interest to people involved in motor racing--especially local club news--plus features. The format has varied from typed newsletter to small newspaper to twenty-page magazine. Business address: 3493 Cahuenga West, Hollywood, Calif. 90068.

FRIDAY NITE HEROES. Indianapolis: 1976-- . Weekly during season.

This newsletter features reports on the late-model and modified racing at Indianapolis Raceway Park. Business office: R.R. 4, Box 70, Lot 184, Mooresville, Ind.

GLEN RACING NEWS. Watkins Glen, N.Y. Irregular.

This newspaper format provides information on racing done on the circuit at Watkins Glen. Business office: P.O. Box 1, Watkins Glen, N.Y. 14891.

GOODYEAR MOTOR SPORTS CLUB NEWSLETTER. Akron, Ohio: Goodyear Tire and Rubber Co., 1975-76. Semimonthly.

This newsletter is no longer published. The Motor Sports Club has ceased operation. The newsletter carried short race and racing related articles. There were a few photographs. Business office: 1144 E. Market St., Akron, Ohio 44316.

HARF NEWSLETTER. Indianapolis: Indianapolis Hoosier Auto Racing Fan Club, n.d. Monthly.

This is one sheet--printed on both sides--that contains news of interest to the membership. There is some racing chit-chat and an occasional photo. It is USAC oriented but other local racing clubs are covered. Business office: c/o Don Wonn, 2640 E. Midland Rd., Indianapolis, Ind. 46227.

I.M.C.A. NEWSLETTER. Vinton, Iowa: International Motor Contest Association. Monthly.

This is the official club publication. It contains club news and race reports. Business office: Box 800, Vinton, Iowa 52349.

LET'S GO RACING. Edited by Dick Conole. College Station, Tex.: Texas World Speedway. Monthly.

This is a mailing piece from Texas World Speedway. It is full of data about Texas World Speedway and other Texas tracks. Business address: TWS, Box AJ, College Station, Tex. 77840.

LONG BEACH GRAND PRIX NEWSLETTER. Long Beach, Calif.: [?]. Irregular.

The Long Beach Grand Prix Association publishes this two or three times prior to the Grand Prix. It is aimed at informing people of the event with ticket prices and other schedule information. There is no charge. Business office: 600 E. Ocean Blvd., Long Beach, Calif. 90802.

MID-OHIO NEWSLETTER. Lexington, Ohio. Three times a year--April, July, Aug.

This newsletter is published by the Mid-Ohio Sports Car Course. There is no cost. Business office: P.O. Box 3008, Lexington, Ohio 44904.

NAMAR NEWS. Marshall, Ind.: National Alliance of Midget Auto Racing. Monthly.

It reports news of interest to the club, competition, and point standings. Business address: Box 234, Marshall, Ind. 47859.

NASCAR NEWSLETTER. Daytona Beach, Fla. Published semimonthly except monthly in November, December, and January.

This is the official newsletter of the National Association for Stock Car Auto Racing. It covers NASCAR racing events and rule changes. Photos are included. Business office: 1801 International Speedway Blvd., Daytona Beach, Fla. 32015.

NATIONAL NATVA ASSOCIATION NEWS. New Bethlehem, Pa. Monthly.

This is the newsletter of the National All-Terrain Vehicle Association. This organization is comprised of owners and dealers of all terrain vehicles. It lists current news, race schedules, and race results. Business office: 342 Broad St., New Bethlehem, Pa. 16242.

THE PROS. Langhorne, Pa. Monthly.

This is a newsletter published by the American Racing Drivers Club, the nation's oldest and largest midget auto racing organization. Business office: 1448 Hollywood Ave., Langhorne, Pa. 19047.

QUARTEREPORTER. Indianapolis: Quarter Midgets of America. Bimonthly.

This newsletter of the Quarter Midgets of America has been in existence for about twelve years. It contains material on club business and reports of racing actions. There are ads to aid quarter midget members. Business office: Betty Parish, 11207 E. Washington St., Indianapolis, Ind. 46229.

RACING PROMOTION MONTHLY. Chanhassen, Minn.: Speedart Publication, 1971-- . Monthly.

This is a trade newsletter for auto racing businessmen--track owners, operators, managers, and PR people. It is primarily idea oriented but deals also with current news and problems of the business or promotional side of racing. Business office: P.O. Box 277, Chanhassen, Minn. 55317.

RMMRA NEWSLETTER. Denver: 1975-- . Irregular.

This is the newsletter of the Rocky Mountain Midget Racing Association. It lists short race summaries, news briefs, and items for sale. Business office: P.O. Box 12005, Denver, Colo. 80212.

ROAD AND TACH. Los Angeles: Santa Monica Sports Car Club. 11 issues yearly.

Since the club is primarily involved in navigational rallying (time, speed, and distance), the newsletter focuses on this material. Most material is of interest to local members. There are good rallying tips for anyone. Business office: 2627 Midvale Ave., Los Angeles, Calif. 90064.

SPEED SPORT PUBLIC RELATIONS NEWSLETTER. Langhorne, Pa.: Ernie Saxton and Associates, 1975-- . Monthly.

This newsletter offers ideas on how to effectively promote the sport of auto racing. Business office: 1448 Hollywood Ave., Langhorne, Pa. 19047.

STOCK REPORT. Eureka, Calif.: Six Rivers Racing Association, n.d. Irregular.

This oversized newsletter is published in January and before each race held at the Redwood Acres Speedway in Eureka, California. It includes news and pictures from the previous race, point standings, future events, letters to the editors and other pertinent information. Business office: P.O. Box 911, Eureka, Calif. 95501.

TECH TIPS. Santa Ana, Calif.: Steve Smith Autosports, 1973-- . Monthly.

This is a monthly question-and-answer technical newsletter designed to be a one-stop informative source for race car problems--be it chassis, handling, or engines. New products and developments are covered each month. Business office: Steve Smith Autosports, P.O. Box 11631, Santa Ana, Calif. 92711.

USAC NEWS. Speedway, Ind. 36 issues yearly.

This publication contains USAC schedules for all divisions, brief summaries of some events, current point standings in all divisions, current announcements, and a feature entitled USAC BULLETIN BOARD which gives brief notices of current happenings in the sport. Examples are driver changes, retirements, awards, and personal notes like marriages and births, and new projects underway. Bussiness address: 4910 W. Sixteenth St., Speedway, Ind. 46224.

VALVOLINE RACE REPORT. Ashland, Ky. 2 to 3 issues yearly.

One issue is produced soon after the Indy 500 and summarizes the race and the success of Valvoline-sponsored drivers. Another issue is published near the end of the calendar year and serves as a year-end wrap-up of Valvoline racing successes in North America. Business office: Valvoline Oil Co., Division of Ashland Oil, Inc., Ashland, Ky. 41101.

VOX VALVOLINE RACE REPORT. Ashland, Ky. Approximately 15 issues yearly.

This is a one-sheet publication featuring races and race drivers affiliated with Valvoline products. The publication is often used as a sales promotional tool at auto races abroad and in Canada. Business office: Valvoline Oil Co., Division of Ashland Oil, Inc., Ashland, Ky. 41101.

Periodicals

YAMAHA COMMUNICATOR. Buena Park, Calif.: Yamaha Motor Corp. Annual.

This is a small tabloid that furnishes information on motorcycles, especially Yamaha's, to motorized dealers. It covers motorcycles, karting, and snowmobile competition. Business office: P.O. Box 6620, Buena Park, Calif. 90622.

Chapter 7
FILM SOURCES

Alabama International Motor Speedway, Box 777, Talladega, Ala. 35160.

They have several documentary types of films including the highly acclaimed FIVE STORIES OF SPEED--TALLADEGA. Films can be borrowed from the speedway.

American Racing Drivers Club, c/o Ernie Saxton, 1448 Hollywood Ave., Langhorne, Pa. 19047.

They have available a 13-1/2-minute color 16mm film on midget auto racing--no sound.

Association Films, 866 Third Ave., New York, N.Y. 10022.

Three motorsports films are available on a free loan basis courtesy of Sears, Roebuck and Co. No. 1, VROOM AT THE TOP examines the racing fortunes of exdriver Roger Penske and his teams in the Indianapolis 500, the Monaco Grand Prix, and the World 600--all on the same day. No. 2 is THE CONTINUING CHALLENGE story of the East African Safari Rally. No. 3 is SEARCH--THE ANATOMY OF AUTO RACING.

Budget Films, 4590 Santa Monica Blvd., Los Angeles, Calif. 90029.

This is a rental agency. It carries a complete line of films including many on motorsports. Color racing films on Baja, the Indy 500, Formula 5000, drag racing, and NASCAR, and additional black-and-white motorsports films with some racing fiction movies are offered.

Champion Spark Plug Company, Film Department, P.O. Box 910, Toledo, Ohio 43661.

Films in the Champion library may be either purchased or borrowed. There is a diversity of subject matter including motorcycle racing, biographies of Buddy Baker and Mark Brelsford, and films on the Indianapolis 500, Road America, and Daytona. A few technical films are also available.

Dick Wallen Productions, P.O. Box 282, Fallbrook, Calif. 92028.

Wallen sells all types of racing films--8mm films, 200 feet each, all color. Several new films are produced each year. Many are on USAC sprints, dirt championship, and midgets. There are some cycle films.

Documentary Productions Incorporated, 6087 Sunset Blvd., Hollywood, Calif. 90028.

They have a stock of 16mm sound and super 8mm sound films on racing cars at Riverside, mid-Ohio, Charlotte, Baja, Bonneville, Indy, Pikes Peak, Ontario, and Phoenix. They also have a film of motorcycle racing at the Catalina Grand Prix and many other titles.

Goodyear Tire and Rubber Company, Public Relations Film Library, Akron, Ohio 44316.

Goodyear lends 16mm sound films without charge to qualified groups. Racing films include several on the Indy 500, biographical pieces on Richard Petty and A.J. Foyt, and a film on drag racing.

H. and H. Productions, 1835 North New Jersey St., Indianapolis, Indiana 46202.

This company has available a 23-minute documentary film on Janet Guthrie, first woman to qualify for and race in the Indianapolis 500. This film THE ULTIMATE CHALLENGE may be purchased or rented.

Indianapolis Motor Speedway Corporation, Speedway, Ind. 46224.

The Indianapolis Motor Speedway has 16mm sound and color films of approximately twenty-five minutes' duration on each of the Indy 500 mile races for the last twenty years. These are available, without charge, on a loan basis to clubs, schools, and civic organizations.

Jim Wilson, Inc., 3003 E. Ninety-Sixth St., Indianapolis, Ind. 46240.

Wilson is involved in television and motion picture production. He does have films on motorsports. Contact the company for details.

Long Beach Grand Prix Association, 600 E. Ocean Blvd., Long Beach Calif. 90802.

They have a three-quarter-inch videotape of the Formula I race held 28 March 1976. This videotape is a duplicate of the CBS television show and as a rule is not loaned out except for special occasions. They also have a 16mm film of the Formula 5000 race which runs approximately twenty minutes and is available on a limited basis.

Modern Talking Picture Service, 2323 New Hyde Park Rd., New Hyde Park, N.Y. 11040.

They have films of all types for free loan including motorsport. At the present time they have a film on Jack Kotchman's hell drivers as well as one on the trip Johnnie Parsons and Paula Murphy took around the world to celebrate America's bicentennial year.

Monroe Auto Equipment Company, International Dr., Monroe, Mich. 48161.

Monroe offers two films at the present time--one that covers the relationship of shock absorbers to various types of drag cars. The other film is on the 1977 Indianapolis 500 mile race. Films are loaned.

Montgomery Ward Auto Club, Box 60100, Chicago, Ill. 60660.

They offer a half-hour film THE NEW YOUNG GIANTS OF RACING on Super Vee competition which is available free to groups upon request.

Pacific Media Distributors, 574 N. Larchmont Blvd., Hollywood, Calif. 90004.

They distribute motorcycle racing films for Yamaha. Films include material on European trials, circuits, motocross, Bonneville Salt Flats, and enduros. There are free loans of films. All are 16mm with color and sound.

Peitscher, Janda/Associates, Inc., 233 N. Michigan Ave., Suite 2208, Chicago, Ill. 60601.

They are the distributors of a film from S-K Tools called TRIPLE CROWN OF RACING which covers action at Indianapolis, Pocono, and Ontario. It is available for cost of postage.

Pyramid Films, Box 1048, Santa Monica, Calif. 90406.

Pyramid sells and rents several motorsports films including THE WILL TO WIN, explaining why people engage in high-risk sports; CATCH THE JOY, a film on dune buggies; and WONDERFUL WORLD OF WHEELS.

Quarter Midgets of America, Edward Wyatt, R.F.D. 2, Box 177, Landenberg, Pa. 19350.

This is a collection of films on quarter midgets. Some are designed primarily for those unfamiliar with the sport and some are designed for members. They will be loaned and are 16mm with both color and sound.

RHR Filmedia Inc., 1212 Avenue of the Americas, New York, N.Y. 10036.

This company distributes for free loan the twenty-minute film THE MAGIC MIDGET which consists mainly of Movietone News footage from the 1930s showing MG racers in action at Brooklands, Mille Miglia, and the Tourist Trophy races in Ireland. It is narrated by three-time World Land Speed Record holder George Eyston.

SCCA Film Library, Sports Car Club of America, Inc., P.O. Box 22476, Denver, Colo. 80222.

SCCA has an extensive library of racing films (black-and-white and color) including technical material, sports car racing at European and American tracks, land speed record films, southern stock car racing, rally films, karting films, East African Safari and dune buggy films, and Indy racing. An unusual entry is BATTLE AGAINST TIME, a Nazi propaganda film showing the mighty Auto Unions and Mercedes teams during the 1937 season in Europe. Two slide programs are also available--one on a driver's school, and the other on flagging and communications at road races.

Score International, 20944 Sherman Way, Suite 115, Canoga Park, Calif. 91303.

SCORE produces films on off-road racing that are used to interest and inform the public.

Sportlite Films, 20 N. Wacker, Chicago, Ill. 60606.

Sportlite sells autosports films--including 500 mile race films through 1976, Daytona 500, and Talladega 500. They have WILBUR SHAW "STAR OF THE SPEEDWAY," a black-and-white silent, super eight film, plus others.

STP Sports Film Library, 1400 W. Commercial Blvd., Ft. Lauderdale, Fla. 33310.

STP has an excellent film library on motorsports. Films are loaned without charge. The collection includes NASCAR, USAC, and land speed films.

Valvoline Oil Company, Division of Ashland Oil, Inc., Ashland, Ky. 41101.

This exciting racing film library covers all aspects of motorsports including Indy 500 races back to 1968, drag racing, Baja, and Grand National. All films are available at no charge from various Valvoline sales offices across the United States and Canada. For the past two years Valvoline has also produced INDY 500 TRACKSIDE REPORTS, a series of ten audio-taped interviews with Indy drivers. These are provided at no charge to interested radio stations.

Chapter 8
OTHER MEDIA

Here we have included those materials which fit into no other category but whose existence should be known to those interested in motorsports productions.

THE BOOK, 330 E. Ninth St., St. Paul, Minn. 55101.

Besides being a relatively complete listing of competition as well as street parts and services for imported cars and race cars, THE BOOK is packed with technical information. Charts, conversion tables, and race track diagrams are all part of this unusual and very useful catalog.

Fleetwood Recording Co., Inc., Revere, Mass. 02151.

Fleetwood produces 8-track tapes. One, GREAT MOMENTS FROM THE INDY 500, brings you such moments as Tony Hulman's "Gentlemen, start your engines," and excerpts of interviews with drivers Bill Vukovich, Rodger Ward, and A.J. Foyt. It is narrated by Sid Collins.

Margrace Corporation, 201 Lincoln Blvd., P.O. Box B, Middlesex, N.J. 08846.

"Auto Rally Cards" are akin to the recipe card sets that have become popular in the last few years. The cards are received on a monthly subscription basis. Many of the card subject areas are racing related such as cards on famous drivers, famous races, and famous racing cars. Motorcycles are also covered. There are photographs and indexing items on the front of each card and data appears on the backs.

Revell, Inc., 4223 Glencoe Ave., Venice, Calif. 90291.

Revell produces material on several of the nation's top drag racers. Film clips are available for promotional purposes as are press kits.

SCCA Film Library, Sports Car Club of America, Inc., P.O. Box 22476, Denver, Colo. 80222.

The library has two slide programs available--one on a driver's school and the other on flagging and communications at road races.

Steve Smith Autosports, Coil-Over Suspension Design Booklet, P.O. Box 11631, Santa Ana, Calif. 92711.

COIL-OVER SUSPENSION DESIGN BOOKLET is an eight-page booklet which provides drawings and photos which demonstrate methods and theories behind the coil-over-shock suspension units. There are three-view scale drawings for mounting coil-over units on late Camaro, Chevelle, square tubing, and MoPar front suspensions, and two-point and three-point rear suspension.

Steve Smith Autosports, THE RACER'S COMPLETE REFERENCE GUIDE, P.O. Box 11631, Santa Ana, Calif. 92711.

THE RACER'S COMPLETE REFERENCE GUIDE is a source book of where to get and how to find all the odd bits and pieces that go into a complicated racing machine. There are many parts catalogs but this book consolidates many different types of needs into one source book.

Steve Smith Autosports, S.S.A. Chassis and Cage Blueprint, P.O. Box 11631, Santa Ana, Calif. 92711.

S.S.A. CHASSIS AND CAGE BLUEPRINT is a kit car design for a complete chassis with roll cage. It includes all necessary parts numbers and material descriptions, plus details, of a unique, simple front frame snout. Plans include two different rear suspensions and two different front snouts and a brochure with chassis photographs.

Steve Smith Autosports, P.O. Box 11631, Santa Ana, Calif. 92711.

Smith produces an assortment of chassis-building blueprints. At the present time the company has a square tube chassis blueprint, a Camaro full frame chassis blueprint, and a Chevelle chassis blueprint. All blueprints include a separate book.

Syndicated Sports Network, Inc., P.O. Box 91, Rushville, Ind. 46173.

ONE WHO DARED: THE LIFE OF AN INDY 500 ROOKIE DURING THE MONTH OF MAY is an excellent stereo LP album that tells the story of rookie Gary Irvin and his attempt to make the 1977 Indy 500. The record is narrated by racing announcer Bill Donnella, and Irvin's experiences are traced by his own recorded comments and those of his mechanic, his car owner Ralph Wilkie, and Indy 500 veteran Tom Bigelow. The record is very well done.

Syndicated Sports Network, Inc., P.O. Box 91, Rushville, Ind. 46173.

The "World of Auto Racing" is an audio presentation of racing coverage that has two formats--one for commercial use on the radio and one home subscription form for the racing fan. The radio show consists of three 5 minute programs a week. The home subscription version is a cassette tape that averages 25 minutes of racing per week. Both formats cover actual race descriptions, driver's meetings, mechanics, official's, and car builder's comments, owners' and sponsors' feelings, and driver interviews. The coverage area is mainly the Midwest with sprint car racing being featured prominently. This is a new fresh approach to motorsport literature.

Valvoline Oil Company, Division of Ashland Oil, Inc., Ashland, Ky. 41101.

Valvoline produces INDY 500 TRACKSIDE REPORTS--a series of ten audio-taped interviews with Indy drivers. These are provided at no charge to interested radio stations.

Wisdom Recordings, P.O. Box 3432, San Angelo, Tex. 76901.

Technical racing tapes by experts are available either on 8-track or cassette. At the present time six tapes are available with more planned. The tapes are 1) SPRINT CARS, covering suspension tuning, gearing, and safety precautions; 2) STOCK CAR RACING, includes engine and chassis setup; 3) SHOCKS, SPRINGS, AND SUSPENSION; 4) TECHNIQUES OF RACING TIRE APPLICATION; 5) INDEPENDENT SUSPENSION. SPRINT AND SUPERMODIFIED; 6) PROMOTIONAL ADVICE, designed to benefit the race organizer or racing team wanting to get more exposure through the news media.

Chapter 9
RACE DRIVERS SCHOOLS

Advanced Institute of Driver Education
P.O. Box 2854
Huntington, W. Va. 25728

This school teaches off-road racing techniques.

Bertil Roos School of Motor Racing
Pocono International Raceway
P.O. Box 500
Mount Pocono, Pa. 18344

Roos uses a Lola T 342. He offers a three-day comprehensive course and a two-day advanced road racing course. The school is approved by SCCA, IMSA, and the Canadian Automobile Sports Club.

Bill Scott Racing School
1420 Springhill Road
McLean, Va. 22101

Scott's school uses two Formula Fords and one Datsun 510 B sedan. Phase I requires no previous experience. Phase II requires recognized racing experience or satisfactory completion of Phase I. An IMSA license is granted to each Phase I graduate. The school is approved by SCCA.

Bob Bondurant School of High Performance Driving
Sears Point International Raceway
Highways 37 and 121
Sonoma, Calif. 95476

Bondorant offers a Grand Prix course (IMSA license issued upon completion), an Advanced Road Racing course, a High Performance Driving course, an Advanced Street and Highway Driving course, a Stunt Driving course, and a Corporate Chauffeurs course (four-day antiterrorist and antikidnapping).

Dallas Motor Racing
2640 Forest Lane
Dallas, Tex. 75234

The circuit used by this school is Dallas Centre.

Fred Opert Racing School
17 Industrial Avenue
Upper Saddle River, N.J. 07458

Gary Bailey Motocross School
P.O. Box 118
Axton, Va. 24054

Bailey's school offers complete motocross training for riders of all ages. The "classroom" is the Lake Sugar Tree Motocross Raceway. The training covers clothing selection, bike setup, safety, braking, starting, jumping, turning, berm technique, track reading, body techniques, performance evaluation, bike maintenance, and physical conditioning.

Jim Fitzgerald School
302 Mount Cross Road
Danville, Va. 24541

Virginia International Raceway is the circuit used by the school.

Jim Russell Racing Driver's School
P.O. Box 911
Rosamond, Calif. 93560

Marblehead Racing Group Race Mechanics Schools
2 S. Barnard Street
Marblehead, Mass. 01945

MRG is a school for race mechanics. It is aimed primarily at Formula Ford drivers who want to do their own mechanical work as well as all aspiring wrench turners. The usual offering is a two-day basic mechanics course--basic racing mechanics. The instructor is Chris Wallach.

Mosport Racing School
88 Queen Street
Bowmanville, Ont.

Nelson Ledges Road Course
Road No. 2
Garrettsville, Ohio 44231

The circuit for this school is Farrettsville.

Pierres Motors Racing
11802 South East Stark Street
Portland, Oreg. 97216

School of High Performance Driving
P.O. Box 59
Somerville, Mass. 02144

Thompson Speedway is used by this school.

Skip Barber School of Performance Driving
1000 Massachusetts Avenue
Boxboro, Mass. 01719

The cars used are Crossle 30-F Formula Fords. Instruction is drawn from Barber's Formula Ford, Formula B, and Formula I experience.

Chapter 10

MOTORSPORT MUSEUMS AND SPECIAL COLLECTIONS

Here we have included museums, libraries, and halls of fame. This list is not comprehensive but attempts to call attention to various types of auto racing archives.

AARWBA Hall of Fame
Ontario Motor Speedway
3901 East "G" Street
Ontario, Calif. 91761

Founded in 1971 and established by the American Auto Racing Writers and Broadcasters Association, this hall of fame was moved to new quarters at the Ontario Motor Speedway in 1976.

Auburn-Cord-Duesenberg Museum
1600 South Wayne Street
P.O. Box 148
Auburn, Ind. 46706

Automobile Reference Collection
Free Library of Philadelphia
Logan Square
Philadelphia, Pa. 19103

Briggs Cunningham Automotive Museum
250 Baker
Costa Mesa, Calif. 92626

The museum is primarily a collection of cars of many types, including competition machinery, collected by Briggs Cunningham.

Citizens Savings Hall of Fame
9800 South Sepulveda Blvd.
Los Angeles, Calif. 90045

Founded in 1936, these museums began life as the Helms Athletic

Foundation and became the Citizens Savings Hall of Fame in 1973. It recognizes many sports including auto racing.

Detroit Public Library
Automotive History Collection
520 Woodward Avenue
Detorit, Mich. 48202

Donington Collection of Single Seater Racing Cars
Castle Donington
Derbyshire, Engl.

There are over sixty-five cars on display, some of which competed on the famous Donington Grand Prix circuit.

Frederick C. Crawford Auto-Aviation Museum
10825 East Boulevard
Cleveland, Ohio 44106

Greenfield Village and Henry Ford Museum
Oakwood Boulevard
Dearborn, Mich. 48121

Harrah's Automobile Collection
P.O. Box 10
Reno, Nev. 89504

Founded in 1948, this is an interesting collection of vintage cars of all types. There is also a library.

Indianapolis Motor Speedway Hall of Fame
c/o Indianapolis Motor Speedway
Speedway, Ind. 46224

The museum's new quarters allow display of approximately sixty cars at any one time. Included are twenty-one race winners. Many other items of interest are also on display.

Joe Weatherly Stock Car Museum
Box 500 Hwy. 34
Darlington, S.C. 29532

Founded in 1965, the museum houses stock cars, photos, trophies, engines, and parts along with a hall of fame of stock car racing people.

MONTAGU MOTOR MUSEUM. See NATIONAL MOTOR MUSEUM.

Murray's Museum
The Bungalow
Snasfell Mountain, Isle of Man

This museum contains an interesting collection of veteran and vintage motorcycles dating from 1902 to 1950. New exhibits are being added.

Museo Dell'Automobile Cario Bisearetti Di Ruffia
No. 40 Corso Unita d' Italia
Turin, Italy

Founded in 1939, the museum moved into its present quarters in 1960. It is an exhibit of cars, chassis, engines, motorcycles, and bicycles. It also contains a library of over four-thousand volumes and many historic archives.

National Motor Museum
Beaulieu
Brockenhurst, Hampshire
Engl.

This is a large museum housing over three-hundred veteran and vintage cars, motorcycles, and pedal cycles. The museum also houses the Transport Reference Library. The collection has also been known as the Montagu Motor Museum, as most of the collection was assembled by Lord Montagu of Beaulieu.

Ormond Garage
79 E. Granada Avenue
Ormond Beach, Fla. 32074

This building saw much early motorsport history being made and is now a national historic site.

Plew's Indy 500 Museum
R.R.2 Box 601
Indianapolis, Ind. 46231

Plew's goal is to preserve the history of all persons and happenings related to the Indianapolis 500. Write first if you want to visit.

Smithsonian Institute
1000 Jefferson Drive SW
Washington, D.C. 20560

Founded in 1846, the exhibits here change so that not all cars owned by the Smithsonian are always on display. One car of particular interest is the turbine car driven by Parnelli Jones in 1967 in the Indianapolis 500.

Totnes Motor Museum
The Quay
Totnes, Devon
Engl.

The museum is a private collection of vintage, sports, and racing cars, most of which are currently raced. The items cover a fifty-year span of motoring. Engines, motorbikes, and motormania are also displayed.

Chapter 11
DIRECTORY OF MAJOR RACING ORGANIZATIONS

All Star Racing League
c/o Islip Speedway
Islip, N.Y. 11751

All-Terrain Vehicle Manufacturers Association (ATVMA)
342 Broad Street
New Bethlehem, Pa. 16242

American Auto Racing Writers and Broadcasters Association (AARWBA)
922 North Pass Avenue
Burbank, Calif. 91505

American Hot Rod Association (AHRA)
3827 West 95th Street
Kansas City, Mo. 64154

American Midget Racing Association
659 Berry Street
Toledo, Ohio 43605

American Motorcycle Drag Racing Association
13221 South Prairie Avenue
Hawthorne, Calif. 90250

American Motorcyclist Association (AMA)
P.O. Box 141
Westerville, Ohio 43081

American Motor Sports Association (AMSA)
P.O. Box 5473
Fresno, Calif.

American Racing Congress
621 West Milham Road
Kalamazoo, Mich. 49002

American Racing Drivers Club (ARDC)
22 Leffets Land
Clark, N.J. 07066

or

62 Lime Kiln Road
Suffern, N.Y. 10901

American Speed Association (ASA)
P.O. Box 2500
Anderson, Ind. 46011

American Three Quarter Midget Racing Association (ATQMRA)
John Little
87 Hazelhurst Avenue
Glen Rock, N.J. 07452

Arizona Racing Association
c/o Warren Franklin
2030 North 37th Drive
Phoenix, Ariz. 85009

Major Racing Organizations

Artgo Racing, Inc.
P.O. Box 355
Libertyville, Ill. 60048

Atlantic Racing Club
Gus Hanson
2440 Terwood Road
Huntington Valley, Pa. 19006

Australian Kart Association
c/o Mrs. J. Hodgetts
7 Ashbourne Avenue
Kingswood
S. Australia 5062

Australian National Drag Racing Association
c/o Mrs. D. Syrmis
P.O. Box 280
Fortitude Valley, Queensland
Australia 4006

Australian Sporting Car Club, Ltd.
P.O. Box 72
Redfern, N.S.W.
Australia 2016

Automobile Competition Committee for the United States, FIA (ACCUS)
Suite 302
1725 K Street NW
Washington, D.C. 20006

Automobile Racing Club of America (ARCA)
Donald Brown
623 Tyron Avenue
Dayton, Ohio 45404

Auto Racing Fraternity Foundation
219 Keith Albee Building
Flushing, N.Y. 11354

Badger Midget Auto Racing Association
R. 3, Box 379
Mukwonago, Wis. 53149

Badger State Dirt Racing Association
Roger Guldan
511 North Walnut
Marshfield, Wis. 54449

Baja De Saddleback
13666 Haror Boulevard
Garden Grove, Calif. 92643

Bay Cities Racing Association
4012 MacArthur Boulevard
Oakland, Calif. 94619

Big Car Racing Association
6881 South Dowing Circle West
Littleton, Colo. 80122

Buckeye Auto Racing Association
179 Thoreau Lane
Xenia, Ohio 45385

California Racing Association (CRA)
c/o Gary Sokola
10391 Maikai Drive
Huntington Beach, Calif. 92646

Cam Car
P.O. Box 534
Vinton, Iowa 52349

Canadian American Modified Racing Association
614 East Decatur
Spokane, Wash. 99207

Canadian Automobile Sport Clubs, Inc.
P.O. Box 97
Weston, Ont. M9N 3M6

Canadian Karting Federation (CKF)
c/o P.O. Box 65-Station A
Weston, Ont. M9N 3M6
Canada

Canadian Race Communications Association (CRCA)
P.O. Box 38-Station Q
Toronto M4T 2L7
Canada

Canadian Racing Drivers Association (CRDA)
P.O. Box 5310-Station A
Toronto M5W 1N6
Canada

Can-Am Midget Racing Club
P.O. Box 34
Kenmore, N.Y. 14217

Car Owners Racing Association (CORA)
2141 Suffolk Lane
Indianapolis, Ind. 46260

Central State Racing Association
c/o Gary Wiesz
P.O. Box 433
Colfax, Calif. 95713

Confederation of Australian Motor Sport
382 Burke Road
Camberwells, Victoria
Australia

Continental Auto Racing Society
Ed Jones
7500 West M-21
Ovid, Mich. 48866

Eastern Motorsports Press Association
1448 Hollywood Avenue
Langhorne, Pa. 19047

Eastern Wisconsin Stock Car, Inc.
P.O. Box 47
Plymouth, Wis. 53073

Evergreen Auto Racing Association
c/o Larry Spoon
608 Harriet West
Montesano, Wash. 98563

Federation Internationale De l'Automobile (FIA)
8 Place de la Concorde
75008 Paris, France

Federation Internationale Motocycliste
26 Avenue de Champel
1206 Geneva, Switzerland

Foreign Stock Car Racing Association
c/o Bob Sternoff
2813 122nd Place, NE
Bellevue, Wash. 98005

Formula Vee International
Box 291
Epharta, Wash. 98823

Greater Inland Empire Stock Car Racing Association
2501 Normandie
Spokane, Wash. 99205

Hoosier Auto Racing Fan Club (HARF)
2640 East Midland
Indianapolis, Ind. 46227

Illinois Mini Stock Racing Association
Larry Zunelli
800 Hermans Lane
Joliet, Ill. 60433

Imperial Valley Dune Buggy Association
Box 151
El Centro, Calif. 92243

Indy Off Roaders, Inc.
R.R. 4, Box 161
Martinsville, Ind. 46151

International Conference of Sports Car Clubs
5425 Sherman Heights Road
Bremerton, Wash. 98310

International Drivers Challenge
P.O. Box 4190
Station "A"
Victoria, B.C. V8X 3X8
Canada

International Hot Rod Association
P.O. Box 3029
Bristol, Tenn. 37620

International Kart Federation
416 South Grand
Covina, Calif. 91724

International Motor Contest Association (IMCA)
P.O. Box 601
421 First Avenue
Vinton, Iowa 52349

International Motor Press Association
230 Valley Road
Montclair, N.J. 07404

International Motor Sports Association (IMSA)
P.O. Box 805
161 Sherman Street
Fairfield, Conn. 06430

Interstates Racing Association
Ray Dropp
445 West Wood Street
Palatine, Ill. 60060

Keystone Auto Racing on Speedway (KARS)
1 Speedway Drive
Mechanicsburg, Pa. 17055

Merrick Auto Racing
2213 Third Avenue
Dodge City, Kans. 67801

Metro Atlantic Quarter Midget Association, Inc.
P.O. Box 148
Powder Springs, Ga. 30073

Mid-America Midget Racing Association
822 East Calhoun Street
Macomb, Ill. 61455

Mid-American Off-Road Association
385 Leaning Tree Road
Greenwood, Ind. 46142

Mid-America Stock Car Racing Association
P.O. Box 3614
Glenstone Station
Springfield, Mo. 65804

Midwestern Council of Sports Car Clubs
Route 1, Box 1566-C
Zion, Ill. 60099

Midwest Race Fans Association
2604 Ellen Avenue
Rockford, Ill. 61103

Midwest Speedways, Inc.
6646 West Fairview Avenue
Milwaukee, Wis. 53213

Midwest Sprint Association
415 Erie Southwest 105
Minneapolis, Minn. 55414

Mighty Midgets of Arizona
4202 West Van Buren
Phoenix, Ariz. 85009

Milwaukee Stock Car Racing Association
1333 North Thirteenth Avenue
West Bend, Wis. 53095

Missouri Valley Midget Racing Association
Publicity Director, P.H. "Bud" Abbott
1414 Jackson Street
Sioux City, Iowa 51105

Modified Stock Car Racing Association
619 "E" Street
Smith Center, Kans. 66967

Motor Sports Press Association (of Northern California)
c/o Harriet Gitting
Box 484
Fremont, Calif. 94537

National Alliance of Midget Auto Racing
Box 234
Marshall, Ind. 47859

National All-Terrain Vehicle Association (NATVA)
342 Broad Street
New Bethlehem, Pa. 16242

National Association for Stock Car Auto Racing (NASCAR)
1801 Speedway Boulevard
P.O. Box K
Daytona Beach, Fla. 32015

National Association of Auto Racing Fan Clubs
3414 Ireland Drive
Indianapolis, Ind. 46236

National Championship Racing Association, Inc.
Bob Walker
1211 South 101 East Avenue
Tulsa, Okla. 74128

National Hot Rod Association
10639 Riverside
North Hollywood, Calif. 91602

National Midget Racing Association, Inc.
c/o Bob McCaw
8521 Kelso
Huntington Beach, Calif. 92646

National Motorsports Press Association
P.O. Box 500
Darlington, S.C. 29532

New England Super Modified Racing Association
R.F.D. 2
Plaistow, N.H. 03865

Northeastern Midget Association (NMA)
R.F.D. 2, Box 226
Plaistow, N.H. 03865

Northeast Wisconsin Tri-Circuit
840 Spruce Street
De Pere, Wis. 54115

Northern Auto Racing Club
911 Washington Street
Calistoga, Calif. 94515

Northern California Racing Association
Box 1411
Lakeport, Calif. 95453

Northern Racing Circuit
James Cocoran
1714 Twelfth Avenue North
Grand Forks, N.Dak. 58201

Northwest Auto Racing Association
c/o Carl Joiner
3809 South East 154th
Portland, Oreg. 97211

Northwest Auto Racing Promoters Association
c/o Mel Spaght
Rt. 3, Box 798
Coos Bay, Oreg. 97450

Northwest Midget Auto Racing Association
3404 Lee Avenue North
Crystal, Minn. 55428

Northwest Push Car Association
c/o Ben Schwartzkopf
7319 South East 118th Drive
Portland, Oreg. 97211

Ohio Midget Auto Racing
P.O. Box 939
Ravenna, Ohio 44266

Ohio Racing Association
Clyde Shaver
6213 Winchester Drive
Seven Hills, Ohio 44141

Pacific Racing Association
c/o Bob Harvey
P.O. Box 805
Wilbur, Oreg. 97494

Quarter Midgets of America
c/o Betty Parish
11207 East Washington
Indianpolis, Ind. 46229

Racewriter's Association
c/o Tom Henderson
244 Fifth Street
Seal Beach, Calif. 90740

Rocky Mountain Midget Racing Association
P.O. Box 12005
Denver, Colo. 80212

Rogue Valley Racing Association
c/o Jack Keck
308 North Main Street
Phoenix, Oreg. 97535

Royal Automobile Club
Motor Sport Division
31 Belgrave Square
London, SW1
Engl.

St. Louis Auto Racing Association
7520 Cory Place
St. Louis, Mo. 63133

or

2457 Shannon
St. Louis, Mo. 63136

Salt Lake Valley Racing Association
c/o Velden Sullivan
323 West 1410 South
Salt Lake City, Utah 84115

Satellites Motorsports Club
c/o Doug Harder
2808 East Sixteenth Avenue
Vancouver, B.C. V5M 2ML
Canada

Score International
20944 Sherman Way
Suite 115
Canoga Park, Calif. 91303

Sierra Auto Racing Association
c/o Mike Lawless
2815 Northridge
Placerville, Calif. 95667

or

7442 Carella Drive
Sacramento, Calif. 95822

Six Rivers Racing Association
c/o Jim Wilson
Rt. 1
Box 185
Eureka, Calif. 95501

Sky Valley Racing Association
c/o Joe Bauer
21407 Highway 9
Woodinville, Wash. 98072

Society of Automotive Engineers (SAE)
400 Commonwealth Drive.
Warrendale, Pa. 15096

Society of Automotive Historians
2105 Stackhouse Drive
Yardley, Pa. 19087

Southeast Midget Auto Racing
7160 Southwest Seventy-first Street
Miami, Fla. 33147

Sports Car Club of America (SCCA)
P.O. Box 22576
Denver, Colo. 80222

Stock Car Auto Racers
c/o Vern Huson
303 South Fifth Street
Kent, Wash. 98031

Sunshine State Midget Association
6140 Thirty-Ninth Avenue, North
St. Petersburg, Fla. 33709

Super Midget Racing Club
7424 Tabor Avenue
Philadelphia, Pa. 19111

Texas Midget Racing Association
12402 Ashcroft
Houston, Tex. 77035

Tri-State Auto Club
Publicity Director: Don Hey
Rt. 5
Bryan, Ohio 43506

Tri-State Circuits, Inc.
P.O. Box 95
South Bend, Ind. 46624

United Auto Racing Association
2112 Leness Lane
Crest Hill, Ill. 60435

United Midget Racing Association
1920 Hiker Trace
Columbus, Ind. 47201

United Racing Club
473 Washington Road
Sayreville, N.J. 08872

United States Auto Club (USAC)
4910 West Sixteenth Street
Speedway, Ind. 46224

United States Racing Club
P.O. Box 1027
Pomona, Calif. 91769

Valley Auto Racing, Inc.
c/o Rex Clark
P.O. Box 1706
Redding, Calif. 96001

Vintage Automobile Racing Association
Canada (VARAC)
Box 65-Station A
Weston, Ont. M9N 3M6
Canada

Washington Association of Demolition
Drivers
c/o Robin Hunt
20302 Eighty-First Avenue, West
Edmonds, Wash. 98040

Washington Midget Racing Association
21904 Eighty-Eighth Avenue, West
Edmonds, Wash. 98020

Washington Racing Association
c/o Rebel Jackson
20404 Eighth Avenue, South
Seattle, Wash. 98142

Western/Eastern Roadracers Association
1742 Addison Street
Philadelphia, PA. 19146

Western Midget Racing Association
12416 Fifty-Second Avenue
Tacoma, Wash. 98446

Western Racing Association
19804 Twenty-Eighth Street, West
Lynnwood, Wash. 98036

Women's Auto Racing Club
Judy Hickey
2204 Johnson Avenue, North West
Cedar Rapids, Iowa 52405

Chapter 12

PUBLISHERS AND DISTRIBUTORS

Hans Abbott
Tiffin, Ohio 44883

Abelard-Schuman
10 E. 53d Street
New York, N.Y. 10022

Harry N. Abrams, Inc.
110 E. 59th Street
New York, N.Y. 10022

Aero Publications, Inc.
329 West Aviation Road
Fallbrook, Calif. 92028

Ian Allan, Ltd.
Terminal Ho
Shepperton, Middlesex TW17 8AS
England

George Allen and Unwin, Ltd.
40 Museum Street
London, WC1A 1LV
England

Arco Publishing Co.
219 Park Avenue South
New York, N.Y. 10003

Aztec Corp.
7002 E. Paseo San Andres
Tucson, Ariz. 85710

Bagnall Publishing Co.
Box 507
Lake Arrowhead, Calif. 92352

Arthur Barker, Ltd.
11 St. John's Hill
London SW11 1XA
England

A.S. Barnes and Co.
P.O. Box 421
Cranbury, N.J. 08512

Barnes and Noble Books
10 E. 53d Street
New York, N.Y. 10022

J.W. Barnes Jr.
Box 323
Scarsdale, N.Y. 10583

Battsford, Ltd.
4 Fitzhardings Street
London W1H 0AH
England

Robert Bentley
872 Massachusetts Avenue
Cambridge, Mass. 02139

Bobbs-Merrill Co.
West 62d Street
Indianapolis, Ind. 46206

Bonanza Books
Division of Outlet Book Co.
One Park Avenue
New York, N.Y. 10016

Bond, Parkhurst Publications
Drawer B
Newfoundland, N.J. 07435

British Book Centre
153 E. 78th Street
New York, N.Y. 10021

Cassel and Co., Ltd.
35 Red Lion Square
London WC1R 4SG
England

Cassell Australia
P.O. Box 52
Camperdown 2050
Australia

Century Services
61 Donegall Street
Belfast BT1
Ireland

Channel Press
Discontinued imprint of Meredith Press

Chilton Book Co.
201 King of Prussia Road
Radnor, Pa. 19089

Classic Motorbooks
P.O. Box 1
Osceola, Wis. 54020

Clymer Publishing
No longer in existence

Collins-World
2080 West 117th Street
Cleveland, Ohio 44111

Coward, McCann and Geoghegan, Inc.
200 Madison Avenue
New York, N.Y. 10016

Cowles Book Co.
Acquired by Henry Regnery Co.

Creative Education Society, Inc.
123 South Broad Street
Mankato, Minn. 56001

Creative Photography Publishers
6229 Fargo Avenue
Las Vegas, Nev. 89107

Thomas Y. Crowell Co.
10 E. 53d Street
New York, N.Y. 10022

Crown Publishers, Inc.
419 Park Avenue South
New York, N.Y. 10016

David and Charles
Brunel Ho
Forde Road
Newton Abbot, Deven TQ12 4PU
England

John Day Co., Inc.
10 East 53d Street
New York, N.Y. 10022

De Paolo Publishing Co.
No longer in existence

Dell Publishing Co.
1 Dag Hammarskjold Plaza
245 East 47th Street
New York, N.Y. 10017

Derbibooks, Inc.
Dist. by Book Sales Inc.
110 Enterprises Avenue
Secaucus, N.J. 07094

Dial Press
1 Dag Hammarskjold Plaza
245 East 47th Street
New York, N.Y. 10017

Discovery Enterprises
P.O. Box 9053
Erie, Pa. 16509

Dodd, Mead and Co.
79 Madison Avenue
New York, N.Y. 10016

Doubleday and Co.
245 Park Avenue
New York, N.Y. 10017

Drake Publishers, Inc.
801 Second Avenue
New York, N.Y. 10017

Dray Publishing Co.
c/o National Speedway Directory
666 Westway NW
Grand Rapids, Mich. 49504

E.P. Dutton and Co.
201 Park Avenue South
New York, N.Y. 10003

Elk Grove Press
1224 West Van Buren Street
Chicago, Ill. 60607

Faber and Faber, Ltd.
3 Queen Square
London WC1N 3AV
England

Farrar, Straus and Giroux, Inc.
19 Union Square West
New York, N.Y. 10003

Follet Publishing Co.
1010 West Washington Boulevard
Chicago, Ill. 60607

G.T. Foulis, Ltd.
Sparkford, Yeovil
Somerset BA 22 7JJ
England

Four Winds Press
Box 126
Bristol, Fla. 32321

Frewin Publishers, Ltd.
5 Goodwins Court
St. Martin's Lane
London WC2N 4LL
England

Funk and Wagnalls Co.
10 East 53d Street
New York, N.Y. 10022

G and J Publishing Co.
1701 West Charleston
Suite 510
Las Vegas, Nev. 89102

Garrard Publishing Company
107 Cherry Street
New Cannaan, Conn. 06840

Goddard Enterprises
Fast/Track
4750-A Mission Boulevard
Ontario, Calif. 91761

Golden Press
850 Third Avenue
New York, N.Y. 10022

Goose and Son, Ltd.
Davey Place 23
Norwich
England

Grenville Publishing Co., Ltd.
Standard House
Bonhill Street
London EC2
England

Grosset and Dunlap
51 Madison Avenue
New York, N.Y. 10010

Haessner Publishing
P.O. Box 89
Newfoundland, N.J. 07435

Robert Hale and Co.
Clerkenwell Ho
45-47 Clerkenwell Green
London, EC1R-OHT
England

Hamlyn Publishing Group, Ltd.
Astronaut House
Hounslow Road
Feltham, Middlesex TWI4 9AR
England

Harper and Row
10 East 53d Street
New York, N.Y. 10022

Harvey House
20 Waterside Plaza
New York, N.Y. 10010

Hawthorn Books, Inc.
260 Madison Avenue
New York, N.Y. 10016

J.H. Haynes and Co., Ltd.
Sparkford, Yeovil,
Somerset BA 22 7JJ
England

William Heinemann, Ltd.
15-16 Queen St.
Mayfair
London W1X 8BE
England

Hippocrene Books, Inc.
171 Madison Avenue
New York, N.Y. 10016

Hi-Torque Publications
16200 Ventura Boulevard
Suite 213
Encino, Calif. 91316

Holt, Rinehart and Winston, Inc.
383 Madison Avenue
New York, N.Y. 10017

Houghton Mifflin Co.
2 Park Street
Boston, Mass. 02107

H.P. Books
P.O. Box 5367
Tucson, Ariz. 85703

Carl Hungness Publishing
P.O. Box 24308-D
Speedway, Ind. 46224

International Publishers Services
114 East 32d Street
New York, N.Y. 10016

Jim Clark Foundation
20 Tudor Street
London EC44 OJS
England

Hugh Keartland Publishers
Nicholson Street
P.O. Box 9221
Johannesburg, South Africa

Pressly R. Keays
6025 St. Clair Avenue
North Hollywood, Calif. 91606

William Kimber and Co., Ltd.
Godolphin Ho
22a Queen Anne's Gate
London SW1H 9AE
England

Lerner Publications
241 First Avenue North
Minneapolis, Minn. 55401

Lionel Leventhal, Ltd.
677 Finchley Road
Childs Hill
London N.W. 2
England

J.B. Lippincott Co.
East Washington Square
Philadelphia, Pa. 19105

Littlebury and Co., Ltd.
THE WORCESTER PRESS
Worcester, England

Lodgemark Press, Ltd.
Bank House, Susan Wood
Chislehurst, Kent BR7 5RD
England

Longmans Canada, Ltd.
55 Barber Greene Road
Don Mills, Ont.
Canada

Lopez Automotive Group
1420 Prince Street
Alexandria, Va. 22314

Lothrop, Lee and Shepard
Imprint of William Morrow
105 Madison Avenue
New York, N.Y. 10016

David McKay Co., Inc.
750 Third Avenue
New York, N.Y. 10017

MacMillan Co.
Riverside, N.J. 08075

MacMillan Publishers, Ltd.
4 Little Essex Street
London WC2R 3LF
England

Bruce Main-Smith
P.O. Box 20
Leatherhead, Sydney
Australia

Mason/Charter
641 Lexington Avenue
New York, N.Y. 10022

Meredith Press
Imprint of Hawthorne Books
260 Madison Avenue
New York, N.Y. 10016

Julian Messner
1230 Avenue of the Americas
New York, N.Y. 10020

William Morrow
105 Madison Avenue
New York, N.Y. 10016

Motorbooks International
P.O. Box 2
729 Prospect Avenue
Osceolo, Wis. 54020

Motor Racing Publications
56 Fitzjames Avenue
Croydon, Surrey CRD 5DD
England

John Murray, Ltd.
50 Albemarle Street
London W1X 4BD
England

National Academy for Police Driving
Route 2
Box 17 BR
Lancaster, Tex. 75146

New Leaf Press
P.O. Box 1045
Harrison, Ariz. 72601

Norquest Enterprises
8620 Crawfordsville Road
Indianapolis, Ind. 46234

W.W. Norton and Co., Inc.
500 Fifth Avenue
New York, N.Y. 10036

Octopus Books, Ltd.
59 Grosvenor Street
London W1X 9DA
England

Stanley Paul and Co., Ltd.
Hutchinson Publishing Group
3 Fitzroy Square
London W1P 6JD
England

J. Philip O'Hara, Inc.
559 West Twenty-Sixth Street
New York, N.Y. 10001

Pelham Books, Ltd.
52 Bedford Square
London WC1B 3EF
England

Performance Marketing, Inc.
3199-A Airport Loop Drive
Costa Mesa, Calif. 92626

Peterson Publishing Co.
6725 Sunset Boulevard
Los Angeles, Calif. 90028

Pocket Books, Inc.
1230 Avenue of the Americas
New York, N.Y. 10020

Post Motor Books
Post Public Box 150
125 South First Avenue
Arcadia, Calif. 91006

Prentice-Hall, Inc.
Englewood Cliffs, N.J. 07632

Princeton Publishing, Inc.
221 Nassau Street
Princeton, N.J. 08540

G.P. Putnam
Send orders to:
390 Murray Hill Parkway
East Rutherford, N.J. 07073

Quadrangle Books
10 East 53d Street
New York, N.Y. 10022

Quazell Technical Publishers
6526 Lanston Street
San Diego, Calif. 92111

Rand McNally and Co.
P.O. Box 7600
Chicago, Ill. 60680

Random House, Inc.
201 East 50th Street
New York, N.Y. 10022

Henry Regnery Co.
180 North Michigan Avenue
Chicago, Ill. 60601

Ridge Press Books
25 West 43d Street
New York, N.Y. 10036

Ruszkiewicz Publishing
Seal Beach, Calif.

S-A Design Publishing Co.
11801 Slauson
Building E
Santa Fe Springs, Calif. 90678

St. Martin's Press
175 Fifth Avenue
New York, N.Y. 10010

Scholastic Book Services
50 West 44th Street
New York, N.Y. 10036

Charles Scribner's Sons
597 Fifth Avenue
New York, N.Y. 10017

Shell-Mex and B.P., Ltd.
Shell Mex Ho Strand
London WC2
England

Lear Siegler, Inc./Fearon
6 Davis Drive
Belmont, Calif. 94002

Steve Smith Autosports
P.O. Box 11631
Santa Ana, Calif. 92711

Souvenir Press, Ltd.
95 Mortimer Street
London, W1N 8HP
England

Speed and Sports Publishing, Ltd.
Bond Street 2A Ealing
London W5
England

Speed Sport Motobooks
Bercourt Ho
51 York Road
Brintford, Middlesex TW8
England

Sphere Books Ltd.
30-32 Gray's Inn Road
London WC1X 8JL
England

Sports Car Press
Dist. by Crown Publishing, Inc.
419 Park Avenue South
New York, N.Y. 10016

Stadia Sports Publishing
381 Fifth Avenue
New York, N.Y. 10016

Patrick Stephens, Ltd.
Bar Hill
Cambridge CB8 8EL
England

Sterling Publishing
2 Park Avenue
New York, N.Y. 10016

Studio Publications, Ltd.
37 Lower Brook Street
Ipswich, Suffolk
England

Superior Books
P.O. Box 4230
Vancouver, Wash. 98662

Jonathan Thompson
23952 Estacia
South Laguna, Calif. 92677

Transport, Ltd.
Fleet Street 161-6
London EC4
England

Trident Press
630 Fifth Avenue
New York, N.Y. 10020

Troll Associates
320 Rte. 17
Mahwah, N.J. 07430

Trust Books
no longer in existence

Two Continents Publishing Group, Ltd.
30 East 42d Street
New York, N.Y. 10017

Viking
625 Madison Avenue
New York, N.Y. 10022

Walck, Inc.
750 Third Avenue
New York, N.Y. 10017

Ward Lock, Ltd.
116 Baker Street
London, W1M 2BB
England

Frederick Warne and Co.
101 Fifth Avenue
New York, N.Y. 10003

Franklin Watts
730 Fifth Avenue
New York, N.Y. 10019

Weidenfeld and Nicolson, Ltd.
11 St. John's Hill
London SW11 1XA
England

Wilton House Gentry, Ltd.
16 Regency Street
London SW1
England

World Publishing Co.
2080 West 117th Street
Cleveland, Ohio 44111

AUTHOR INDEX

This index includes all authors, editors, compilers, and other contributors cited in the text. It is alphabetized letter by letter.

A

B

C

Q

R

S

T

TITLE INDEX

This index includes all titles of books (titles of films and tapes are also included) which are cited in the text. Some lengthy titles have been shortened. This index is alphabetized letter by letter.

A

B

C

G

H

I

M

N

S

T

U

V

W

Y

SUBJECT INDEX

This index is alphabetized letter by letter.

C

D

Q

R

S